NO QUARTER

NO QUARTER

by

KONSTANTIN SIMONOV

Correspondent of RED STAR

★★

1943

L. B. FISCHER · NEW YORK

NO QUARTER

The Turn of the Tide

★★

It was june 24, 1941. The train—for some reason it was composed of short-run cars without corridors—left the darkened platform of a Belorussian station. The station was lit by dim blue lamps—to which most of us were not yet accustomed. The train was bound for Minsk. Most of its passengers were officers returning from leave. This was the third day of the war, and all of them were hurrying westward, to the front.

At my side sat a tank corps colonel, a man of small stature and greying hair with the order of Lenin on his tunic. He was accompanied by his son, who, if I remember correctly, was called Misha. The People's Commissariat for Defense had given the father permission to take his sixteen-year-old boy with him to the front as a volunteer. Father and son resembled each other; both were short and stocky, with stubborn chins and hard, grey eyes.

The train went only as far as Borisov. Ahead of us were torn-up tracks, the Germans, the unknown.

In a wood near Borisov, on the bank of the Berezina, were gathered a few thousand officers and Red Army men returning to their units. These units had been fighting further west, but between them and us were the Germans who had unexpectedly broken through in the direction of Borisov.

Wave after wave of roaring German planes bombed us and strafed us from dawn to sunset; in front of us heavy guns thundered. We all belonged to different units, we did not know one another and we had no idea what was happening at the front. But one man rallied this heterogeneous mass and gave each of us something useful to do. The soul and heart of the group gathered in the woods near Borisov turned out to be the little colonel who had sat beside me in the train. He was the first to utter the words: "Take up defensive positions." He assembled the senior officers around him, took an inventory of our weapons, divided our men into companies and platoons. As a result, a formless crowd became an army.

Some big guns were found, as well as a few machine guns. Some of the men were sent back to Borisov to get more equipment. We dug trenches and shelters, chose the best positions we could find and manned them. All kinds of people were there. On my left an artillery captain and a military judge were lying with their rifles; on my right were two civilians, truck drivers.

I shall never forget the colonel's son. The boy did all sorts of jobs. Without ever removing his rifle from his back, he ran errands, brought us food, water and cartridges and, in his rare free moments, cast admiring glances at his father. The boy was happy to be a soldier and proud that it was his father who at this difficult moment had proved the most resolute of all the grown-ups in uniform.

He was right to be proud of his father. The colonel acted as though nothing extraordinary had happened, as though he were commanding, not a group of people who had never seen one another, but a regular regiment which had worked under him for at least three years. He issued orders in a calm, somewhat flat voice. But there was an iron note in that voice, and everyone obeyed him. His name was mentioned to me a few times, but later I forgot it.

The following day I left the colonel and never saw him again.

In November, I was at the Karelian front, on the Rybachi Peninsula. We had just received a very much delayed batch of Moscow newspapers. In one of them, on the front page, was a picture with the following caption: "Colonel Liziukov, Commander of the 1st Guards Motorized Rifle Division, Hero of the Soviet Union, receives the Guards' flag." Before the drawn-up troops, with a flag in his hands, stood a colonel in a winter overcoat. A little stocky man, with a stubborn chin. . . .

I recognized him as the hero of the woods below Borisov, last June. And I recalled the name I had forgotten—Colonel Liziukov. I don't know why I had such a strong desire to see his son in the picture, standing beside his father, just as he had stood beside him then, in June. . . .

I evoked all this with particular clarity in December when, having traveled over many roads near the Western front, I saw the marks of the German retreat, which were now being ruthlessly destroyed. Today, when we have learned how to be victorious, we may permit ourselves to recall what was too hard to recall in the earlier days of the war. Today I can evoke those first two hard months, June and July, our first cruel defeats and lessons, the blood-drenched roads along which we retreated and along which we are today moving back. And today we are filled with particular pride and gratitude when we think of the people who were then the soul of our troops. When we looked at such people in those hard days we realized that all our set-backs were but a phase, that we would soon be victorious and return to the lands we had lost, that we would surely be victorious and return. We did not know when, but looking at them, we knew we would return some day, without fail.

When Russia was devastated by the Tartar invasion, when her cities were burned and drowned in blood, the people expressed their grief and their lamentations in immortal songs. All the chronicles, those of Novgorod, Suzdal, Vladimir, Riazan, preserved these songs and, along with them, the story of the hero of Riazan, Evpati Kolovrat. Finding his native city burned upon his return from an expedition he pursued the countless Tartar army with a small body-guard. Having caught up with the enemy, he killed a large number of them and perished heroically with his guards in an uneven battle.

The Tartars were finally driven out, the Russians were victorious at the decisive battle of Kulikovo, but along with the names of the victorious leaders, like Dmitri Donskoi, the memory of the people preserved the name of Evpati Kolovrat, the popular hero of the first sorrowful days of the Tartar invasion. They held his name dear because in those hard and bloody times his exploit was not only a comfort, not only a matter of pride, but a guarantee of ultimate victory.

Times and enemies have changed—I am not trying to draw historical parallels—but the people have not changed. They are still manly when faced with an ordeal and they still cherish those who during such an ordeal display purity of soul and strength of spirit.

So it will be again. The names of the conquerors will not overshadow the names of the heroes of the battles of June, July and August in the memory of our people. I know that in the days of our worst defeats, we newspapermen, whose mission it was to tell the people what was taking place at the front, sought out men and women whose exploits were an assurance of victory—and we found many of them. They were army Bolsheviks, soldiers of the Stalin school, who during the difficult days took all the burden of the war on their shoulders.

I remember a field near Mogilev. A single wooden bridge led from the eastern to the western bank of the Dnieper. There was not a single gun or anti-aircraft gun on it. We crossed over to the west bank and joined the regiment defending Mogilev. A hard, bloody battle took place that day. Our regiment destroyed forty German tanks, but suffered severe losses. When night came, we talked with Colonel Kutepov, the commander of the regiment. He was a very tall, thin, rather awkward man, who had served in the army for many years and yet looked as if he had discarded his civilian clothes only yesterday. At the most difficult moments, his unshaven, tired, really mortally tired, face was suddenly lit up by a gentle, almost childlike smile.

We told him about the bridge, which had no anti-aircraft guns. We told him that if the Germans managed to destroy it with a bomb, he and his regiment would be cut off on this side of the Dnieper.

"Well, what of it?"—and Kutepov suddenly smiled his childlike smile—"What of it?" he repeated in a low gentle voice, as though talking about something very unimportant. "Let them bomb it. Even if the others retreat, we have made up our mind to remain here and die, the whole regiment has discussed it and decided it that way."

[8]

I can still see Kutepov standing there at headquarters, when a liaison man ran up to him.

"Comrade Colonel, there are thirty tanks on our right flank," he said, panting.

"What? Where are there tanks?" cried one of the officers standing beside the colonel. He had heard only the word "tanks," but not their number.

"Tanks? Oh, there are about three lousy little ones, on the right flank," said Kutepov, smiling.

To this very day I can see his worried eyes and his smile. His eyes were worried, because there were thirty tanks on the right flank and because something had to be done about it. And he smiled, because his aide was about to go to the left flank and it was better for him to believe that there were not thirty, but three tanks on the right flank.

I don't know whether or not this deception was wrong from a military point of view, but that minute, as I looked at him, I realized that we would be victorious, without fail, that it could not be otherwise.

How the roads leading to the front have changed! I will never forget the Minsk highway along which walked the refugees, in endless files. They walked dressed in any kind of clothing, sometimes in what they had been wearing when roused out of their beds. They carried little bundles of food in their hands, and so tiny were these bundles that it was impossible to imagine what they had been eating during the five, ten and sometimes fifteen days they had spent on the roads.

Above the highway at that time roared German planes. Today they no longer fly as they did then, they don't dare. But in those early days of the war they flew low as though trying to run people over, crush them with their wheels. They bombed and strafed the road. Driven off the bloodsoaked highway the refugees sought shelter in the woods and continued walking on both sides of the road, at a distance of a hundred feet. Next day the Germans realized this, and their planes, instead of following the road, began to fly either side of it, loosing a hail of bombs where, according to their calculations, the refugees were now walking.

I recall villages where in those days people asked us: "You won't let the Germans get this far, will you?" And they looked into our eyes.

And it seemed easier to die than to answer that question. For many months I could not speak of all this because it was too painful; I can evoke it now because I have just traveled westward along many of the same roads that were once the path of our retreat to the east.

Once again refugees move along these roads, but this time they are not leaving, they are returning. Only in time of crisis do you realize the power of a man's native soil, the irresistible desire to come back of people who have been forced to leave their homes. They do not wait till all is quiet; they follow on the heels of our armies. They return before the danger is over, before the fires have been put out, while the thunder of guns can still be heard. They refuse to lose even a single day. They want to get back to their homes the very day our soldiers recapture them.

In time of war, army men are supposed to know more than civilians, they must answer all questions, they dare not use the excuse that they are not informed. The people who toil along the roads love to ask questions, they want to know many many things, and they want to know them immediately, without delay.

They asked questions in June 1941 and they asked questions in December. But how different these questions were now. I recall that in July we passed through Shklov. The refugees on the roads were frightened by every passing car. They saw a few cars going toward them, in a westerly direction. They stopped them and asked: "Perhaps we shouldn't leave, perhaps the Germans won't come here?" And their eyes shone with hope. But then again military vehicles went by going east, and the refugees followed them with despair in their eyes. They urged on their horses, they hurried, they asked where they should go: to Roslavl, or farther on?

December. The same roads. In the town of Odoev we were surrounded by a group of people who had just returned. They asked us when Mtsensk would be recaptured and when Belev would be taken. They had left relatives there and knew that if these relatives were still alive they would soon see them again. They felt that Belev would be retaken without fail, all they wanted to know was when it would be retaken. Soon, we say, soon. We, too, believe it. And then they began to ask questions about Kaluga, about Orel, about other cities.

"When?" they asked over and over again looking at the Red Army men with unshakable faith. And under these looks, our cavalrymen involuntarily spurred their horses and trotted off toward the west.

One night in November, at the headquarters of our far northern army, where the incandescent northern lights illumined half the sky, a member of the special section, who had gone out with me into the cold to smoke and have a breath of air, suddenly, as though remembering something, said to me in a joyful voice: "You know, there will soon be something interesting for you. We've captured three German officers."

"What are their ranks?" I asked.

"I don't know yet."

"Haven't they arrived at headquarters yet?"

"No."

"They're still with the regiment?"

"No. You see . . ." my informant seemed embarrassed. "You see, the fact is that these prisoners haven't arrived at all, they're still behind the German lines. They were captured forty miles behind the German lines, between their army corps and our divisional headquarters. Fifteen of our frontier guards have penetrated that far and it is they who have taken the prisoners. They radioed that they are bringing us three officers and that they will cross the lines in two or three days. So we'll have to wait a little."

I recall this incident now because, more than a bold coup by a handful of brave men, it was a symbol of the new victorious spirit which is growing stronger in our army from month to month. In July we had not taken German prisoners forty miles beyond our front lines. In November we began taking them. And what matters is not so much that such things were done, as that they were considered normal, that they aroused no particular surprise.

Three days later I saw these three German officers. They were brought in wearing extra felt boots which our men had taken with them. They were given felt boots not out of excessive kindness on our part, but simply because it was easier to get them here that way. These officers, from the famous Kritt Alpine Brigade, were a rather lamentable sight. They had not yet fought in our way, they had not yet become accustomed to our new methods or to being taken prisoner. They were told that in the very near future many of their colleagues would have to become accustomed to life in prison camps. They were silent; and they were silent not out of pride or outraged dignity, as they had been in the beginning, but simply because they had nothing to say, because they had lost all their will-power and their minds were a blank.

How these "invincible" soldiers had changed in six months! In July it was hard to distinguish the brave ones from the cowards. At that time an all-pervading insolence overshadowed their other human qualities. As soon as they saw that they were not to be beaten up

[13]

or shot when taken prisoner, they gave themselves all sorts of airs. They thought that the war would be over in two weeks, that their stay in a Russian prison camp was an enforced rest, so to speak, and that they were being treated humanely only from fear of reprisals later on.

They are different now. Some of them tremble and weep and, choking convulsively over their words, tell everything they know; others—an insignificant minority—are wrapped in despair and maintain a gloomy silence. In their days of defeat this army of overbearing braggarts has changed, as one might expect troops to change who have been accustomed to easy victories and now suffer defeat for the first time.

The Germans are retreating. They are fighting back, but they are retreating. They snap at us whenever they can, but they must flee before our might.

On the general's table lay an operational map. I had seen many such maps during this war, but how different they were now! Do you remember the maps in July, August, October? There were big blue arrows on them, and red half-circles. Today, there are red arrows on them, drawn in a bold resolute hand, and blue circles. The Germans are retreating. The red arrow is moving farther and farther away from Moscow, westward, and entering deeper and deeper into the blue enemy lines, cutting their concentrations to pieces, isolating them. The blue semi-circles are smaller and smaller, more and more often they are divided into regiments, battalions, companies.

[14]

I examined one of these maps. Our troops had driven a deep, thirty-mile wedge into the disposition of the retreating German divisions. Behind our men entire German regiments were still scattered, every day our roads were still being cut by handfuls of automatic riflemen, but our divisions moved steadily forward knowing that they would eventually surround and exterminate the Germans. For a minute I tried to visualize this map as it looked in July or August. If we had looked at it then, we would have thought that here, in this sector, not the Germans were surrounded but we ourselves!

A surrounding army is always to a certain extent itself surrounded—everybody knows that. But what is important is, not which side has more regiments and divisions, but who is on the offensive, who considers himself surrounding or surrounded. Something has taken place on this front which was much more important than the capture of ten or twenty towns or villages; a tremendous, a magnificent change in the psychology of our army and our individual soldiers. Our army had learned to defeat the Germans. And even when our regiments found themselves in difficulties, when the issue of a battle seemed to hang in the balance, they felt sure that they would win just the same and they continued to attack and strike severe blows at the enemy.

A similar change in the opposite sense had taken place in the German army. They felt themselves surrounded, they retreated, they continually tried to

[15]

shorten their lines, they feared every handful of men who penetrated behind their positions, firmly believing that the Germans could be defeated.

A report was brought to the colonel to the effect that a company of German automatic riflemen had appeared at his rear. "Well," he said, "some of our men will get behind them and destroy them; our business is to move forward, always forward." And without even mentioning this subject again, he gave the order to continue our advance.

For the enemy must be smashed, and no matter what happens, he will be smashed. Every one of our men knows this, and what is more important, knows it with all his heart. Our men were pursuing the Germans on this front and they will continue to pursue and surround them everywhere, on the roads and in the narrow mountain passes and on wintry fields where cars get mired, where your legs get stuck in the snow, where it is almost impossible to move. When people move forward, they are lifted up by some mysterious force, they acquire additional lungs. We had forced our will on the Germans, we were masters of the situation. They would try to get out of the encirclement through burning villages, through impassable thickets, and tomorrow they would freeze by the hundreds where today they were freezing by the dozens. And they would be killed not only with automatic rifles and guns, they would be killed along the roads with picks and pitchforks by women and old men—just as on these same roads other intruders were killed in 1812.

[16]

And let them not expect mercy. We have learned to be victorious, but we have learned it at too high and cruel a price to give any quarter to the enemy.

Let the enemy remember this and let him remember that the phrase of our commander-in-chief, "a war of extermination," means for the rank-and-file Red soldier not only a fighting slogan, not only words, but a dead German lying on the snow with a bayonet stuck through his throat, and another dead German and still another—as many dead Germans as we shall have strength to kill in our short lives.

Covering Units

★★

"OUR COVERING UNITS have passed over to the offensive and are holding the enemy pending the approach of our main forces." More than once we have read this modest matter-of-fact sentence in the communiqués issued by the Information Bureau. But very few people know the reality behind this brief sentence, the daring exploits, the iron tenacity that are implied in the simple words, "holding the enemy pending the approach of our main forces."

Military language is always laconic. An order may say: "Hold the enemy." But in our army, "hold" means "hold at any cost," and "fight" means "fight to the last drop of blood."

The covering units were the first to receive the

blows of the enemy, the first to feel out his strategy and tactics, the first to develop, while fighting him, the new methods necessary to defeat him. They stopped the enemy, although sometimes they committed costly errors; then, in correcting these errors, they accumulated new fighting experience which the whole army will eventually use to rout the invaders. While the covering units held back the enemy, our main forces were able to concentrate and deploy, were able, above all, to win time—time, of which the real price is learned only on the battlefield.

Once an army has deployed, the covering units are brought to the rear, a few dozen miles behind the first lines. But in this war there is no precise limit between the front and the rear.

At night, when the camp was silent, one could hear the distant cannonade of heavy guns—our long-range artillery. When dark began to fall, white reflections flashed through the woods, a dot, a dash, a dot, a dash— these were made by German diversionist groups trying to communicate with each other or to signal to their aircraft.

Then our little flares would go off quickly—our reconnaissance had learned to work accurately. After the third dash, the signalman was usually discovered.

When I arrived at the Western front the covering units were being replenished, brought up to full strength after their losses. New guns and machine guns replaced the weapons which had been crippled in severe battles.

[19]

But if you talked with the commanders and common soldiers of such covering units which had just been at the front lines, losses were the subject mentioned least often; our men spoke of their battle experiences, of the enemy's weak points, of the new techniques they had worked out in battle and that they were now using against him. And when they evoked their lost comrades, they did not evoke them simply to bemoan their loss, but to discuss their conduct on the battlefield, the fighting experience which they had transmitted to the others at the cost of their lives.

On June 22, 1941, the Nth Rifle Regiment, along with other regiments of the division, was put on a war footing, and in twenty-one hours performed a march of fifty miles. Under fire from the enemy's aircraft, the regiment loaded its men and equipment on trucks and at daybreak arrived at the concentration point. Only a few miles now separated our regiment from an approaching enemy tank division. Deploying as they moved up, the regiment occupied defensive positions along the sloping banks of the S— River. To give our men an opportunity to entrench themselves and the howitzer brigade time to take up advantageous firing positions, the 2nd Battalion was thrown forward, entrusted with the honorable task of receiving the first blows of the enemy.

It is hard to dislodge steadfast infantrymen from their positions, if they have had time to dig themselves in, even hastily; it is hard, even if a whole tank division is launched against one regiment. The Germans knew this as well as ourselves, and while the regiment was engaged in digging itself in, every fifteen minutes enemy planes dove over it with a roar. But the Germans' hope of creating a panic, of slowing up our defensive work was thwarted. Taking cover behind trees, dropping flat on the ground and getting up again, our men coolly and rapidly continued their preparations. There was no running around, no disorderly firing from rifles; everyone did his job; the infantrymen dug in and the anti-aircraft gunners tended their guns. And it must be said that in this first battle our anti-aircraft batteries gave a rather good account of themselves. Calmly waiting for the precise moment when the enemy planes began to dive, our heavy caliber anti-aircraft machine guns sent their shells straight into the bombing squadron. One after another, three burning Stukas crashed into the trees with a deafening noise.

By then the 2nd Battalion had accepted an uneven fight. Its anti-tank guns fired point-blank at the tanks. Retreating from one exposed position to another, our machine gunners, by deftly directed fire, tried to isolate the enemy infantry from their tanks, forcing them to drop on the ground, and keep their heads down. One tank took fire, then a second, a third and a fourth; the other machines now moved more slowly than at the beginning, stopping at intervals to take a shot at our anti-tank guns and thus give the German infantry, which had not displayed any particular courage under fire, time to get close to them.

In the meantime our battalion, having performed its

[21]

task of delaying the enemy, gradually retreated toward the left flank of the regiment.

By four o'clock in the afternoon, the battle had flared up along the entire front of the regiment. From the number of the attacking tanks it was now clear that an entire motorized division had been thrown against us. The narrow strip of the river, spanned by a single bridge, separated us from the enemy. The tanks drove up to the river bank and concentrated near the bridge, but were prevented from crossing it by our furious artillery barrage. The German infantry, assembled at the edge of the woods, was trying to reach the bank by short runs and ford the river.

A few other tanks took fire. From our positions we had a good view of the German infantrymen. Our machine-gun fire had slowed them up, but they attempted to move forward in spite of it. But when the tanks went up like torches to right and to left, they immediately dropped to the ground, and the officers had a hard time making them get up again. Apparently the Nazis' faith in the steel machines that until then had won them so many easy victories had its negative side.

The tanks took fire, one after another. The German infantry was not accustomed to this, they were afraid to advance without the support of their armor. They wanted the tanks to go first. Again tanks were sent ahead and concentrated near the bridge; and again they were set ablaze.

Then the enemy brought up artillery to support his

tanks. Massing it along the river, he began to hunt out our anti-tank guns. When night fell, by the combined efforts of his artillery and tanks, he had succeeded in knocking out half of our guns. But it is not for nothing that the Russian artillery is famous. Our remaining guns discovered the emplacements of the enemy batteries and by night their accurate fire destroyed eighteen cannon and set sixteen tanks ablaze. Working with the artillery, our machine-gunners directed their fire at the observation slits of the Nazi tanks and blinded the enemy.

But our losses finally began to tell. Our fire grew less concentrated, and detachments of German infantry taking advantage of this managed to crawl to the brink of the river and began to ford it. Having noticed this maneuver, the 2nd Company of our regiment left cover and launched a furious counter-attack. The Germans flinched before our bayonets and hurriedly retreated toward the opposite bank.

When night fell, there was a lull for a few minutes. But at exactly 10:00 P.M. the enemy, having apparently given up his attempt to take our positions by direct assault, moved up his howitzers and opened a veritable hurricane of fire. A dense, flaming wall seemed to be moving from the bank of the river toward the woods and from the flanks to the center of our positions. It took iron grit to hold our ground under this barrage and keenly to observe every movement of the enemy. Under cover of this wall of fire, the German infantry began to cross the river and to mass on our side

[23]

of it. Exactly at midnight, the Germans aimed their artillery barrage beyond our front lines. Convinced that our units had been destroyed and demoralized by the two hours' bombardment, they at last decided to attack.

But exactly at midnight the commander of our regiment, too, having decided not to wait for the German attack, gathered all his forces together, assembled the men who had survived the barrage, exhorted them to keep up the good fight and with a loud "hurrah" took the Germans who had crossed the river entirely by surprise. Thrown into disorder, some wading, some swimming, they turned back, flinching before a bayonet battle. But many of them were forced to experience the force of our bayonets, and never succeeded in getting across.

Thus ended this hard day. The German tank division was stopped for twelve hours and lost thirty tanks and eighteen guns. Our losses, too, were serious. But in spite of them, our soldiers felt victorious that night. The crippled German tanks and guns, the killed German infantrymen, were only half of our victory. The other half was our gain of time. Twelve hours of battle time! The men knew that behind them our main forces were deploying and taking advantage of the twelve hours we had won in a bloody battle.

By daybreak our regiment left the woods, which had been mutilated by shells and dug up with bombs. The regiment withdrew to occupy a new defensive line, where it was to fight another fierce and heroic battle the following day.

And the morning communiqué of the Soviet Information Bureau contained this terse line: "In the course of the past day our covering units held the enemy attack until the approach of our main forces."

Routine Day

IT IS WARMER NOW. The shell craters along the roads are thawed and muddy. Flocks of black ravens fly over German birch crosses recalling the December battles, and the gray turrets of shattered German tanks protrude from the snow.

On the hillside, with its panorama of white hills and blue glades, a monument has been erected: a tin star and a tablet on which the thoughtful but hurried hand of a man returning to battle inscribed tersely: "In memory of Senior Lieutenant Bondarenko and Junior Lieutenant Gavrish who died heroically in the battles near Square Grove on March 27. Farewell, our companions-in-arms! Forward and westward!"

From the lofty monument there is a good view of

the wintry landscape. Perhaps the soldiers who built it wanted their dead comrades to look on as their regiment continued its march westward across the snowy Russian plains. In front of the hill there are several little forests, Square Grove, near which Bondarenko and Gavrish fell in battle, and others, Birch, Oak, Curved, Turtle and Leg Groves. They were not called by these names before, nor will they be in the future; they are in fact small nameless glades and groves. Their godfathers were the commanders of the regiments who fought here for every clump of trees and every grove. These little woods are the scenes of daily battles. Their new names appear every night in divisional reports; sometimes they are even mentioned in army communiqués.

Twenty-four hours have passed—twenty-four hours of battle, amid the muffled thud of mine explosions, the crash of trees uprooted by tanks, the brief crackle of bullets ricocheting from birch trunks.

7:00 P.M. Major Gritsenko's regiment has just captured the little grove with the unpleasant name of Appendicitis. This grove was a wedge driven into our positions. The Germans entrenched themselves in it. For several days it made life unpleasant for our regiment. It was given the medical name of "appendicitis," and we treated it like an infected appendix; we outflanked it and cut it off.

Now it is quiet in the grove; the half-dozen fortified dugouts, the dead German soldiers scattered in various attitudes under the white Russian birches—

all are silent. One of the corpses is sitting on the snow with his arms around a birch, and I have to fight against my impulse to tear these unclean hands from the tree to which they are clinging. There are two piles of corpses. They were killed yesterday and the day before, and apparently the Germans who had remained alive, despairing of their efforts to break out of our encirclement, dragged them here to bury or burn them.

Yes, they fight with wolfish tenacity. And to conquer them day after day means, on every yard of ground, to break their incredible stubbornness by our steady pressure, day after day. In February, 1942, Hitler made each of his soldiers swear that he would not retreat one yard without his personal order. This appeal to the soldier's fighting spirit proved, however, ineffectual. Then the German High Command announced that decorations formerly distributed sparingly would now be given for each wound, each scratch. But this appeal to vanity also proved ineffectual. Then the German command declared that every attempt to withdraw would be punished by immediate execution. This was an appeal to fear. All these measures, combined with the long habit of unquestioning obedience, produced a feeling of hopelessness among the Germans, nailed them to the snowy ground, left them with no other alternative than to stay till the end.

We kill many of them, but a pile of corpses such as we saw today is rather rare. As a rule, the Germans carry their dead to the rear. At first sight this may seem a manifestation of soldierly solidarity—after all the instinct of comradeship is found even among beasts. But the last prisoners we took here give us a different explanation of this practice. German soldiers are permitted to retreat only if they are carrying a dead or wounded comrade. When under fire, they wait for the death of a comrade, so as to find safety for a time by carrying his body to the rear. The dead give the living a reprieve from death.

Dusk. The trunks of the birches are blue now. The snowdrifts ahead of our trenches merge with the surrounding fields. The black embrasures in the German dugouts are camouflaged with white handkerchiefs and rags. Everything is white, invisible.

9:00 P.M. This is the darkest hour. The moon has not yet risen. Our nerves are strained to the limit. All of us expect a German counter-attack. But the rattle of machine-gun fire that breaks out is not from the west where we expected it, but from behind our lines, from the grove we captured today. Major Gritsenko details a company to the rear with the order to mop up the grove again.

By daybreak, our detachment, after a cautious march, reaches the edge of the woods. One of our soldiers is cut down by a sudden burst of submachine-gun fire. He falls without a sound. His comrades next to him move silently forward, running from tree to tree, dropping to the ground and rising again. The enemy fire grows more intense. In a glade surrounded by dense woods, a considerable group of Germans who have remained behind dig themselves in. German tommy guns keep firing volley after short volley. In the cold, bluish light of the dawn, our troops can see occasional movements behind the low, snow-covered parapets of the German trenches.

It is impossible to continue our advance into Oak Grove without first destroying these soldiers who have dug themselves in behind our lines. And it is not possible to postpone our attack on Oak Grove.

Our assault of the German positions at our rear is brief and fearless. Perhaps because of its impetus, it does not cost us too many casualties. The enemy is dislodged from his hastily dug trenches, dispersed and wiped out. Altogether there are fifty dead: forty-nine soldiers and one *Oberleutnant*. Yesterday they withdrew from the grove, hoping to wait here and later break through to their own lines. Actually the number of dead is not forty-nine but forty-five. When our soldiers test the "corpses" with bayonets, four Germans stand up and raise their hands.

By 11:00 P.M. Appendicitis has been cleaned out. Oak Grove still remains to be taken. After more than twelve hours of strenuous fighting a liaison officer approaches one of the German dugouts which now serves as Major Gritsenko's command post and reports that our tanks have arrived. The major goes out with him. The tanks stand at the edge of the woods, heavy, grayish machines that smash birch trees like matches. We know from our scouts that there are

two lines of deep trenches ahead of us, with three to
four dozen fortified dugouts. The approaches to them
are mined.

The major has organized small storm groups of six
to seven men each. Three such groups are assigned to
each tank, two to its sides, one behind. At the edge
of the woods, beside the tanks, stand light 45-milli-
meter guns ready for action. Everything has been
taken care of. Trench mortars placed on wide ski-
runners are dragged to forward positions. It is exactly
noon. The midday sun shines through the trees, and if
it were not for the dull explosions of mortar shells
overhead, the woods would seem to be at peace.

The storm groups start to move, led by the sappers; the tanks rumble along in between. The soldiers
take fifty, sixty, eighty steps. The Germans are silent.
Then one of them can't restrain himself any longer.
From behind a high, snowy parapet a machine gun
begins to rattle. Our storm groups take over. The tank
turns its gun, stops and hurls a shell, then another,
then a third, at the machine gun which has revealed
its position. Snow and smashed wooden planks fly into
the air. The Germans take cover; our storm group
gets up and dashes another thirty steps forward.
Then, the same thing is repeated: machine-gun volleys from the next dugout, a short advance by our
tank, a few shells, and snow and planks flying in the
air.

The Germans retreat along the trenches, but our
tank, sometimes steering its way among the trees,

sometimes smashing over them, moves along the trenches, hurling shell after shell into them. At first the Germans, after running a few steps in their trench, pierce a hole in the snowy parapet and fire at our infantry with tommy guns. But now many are forced to leap out of one trench and, sinking into the snow up to their waists, try to reach the next. During these intervals, our soldiers advancing with the tank rise from the ground, and one after another the German grey coats form dark spots on the snow.

In the grove the air itself seems to be whistling, bullets cut into trees, ricochet and fall spent on the snow. The first line of German trenches is captured. With the help of the infantry, our artillerymen make a path through the soft spring snow, drag their guns by hand after the tanks, at every stop firing on the dugouts and blockhouses. We are so close now that the German trench mortars set up at the edge of the woods cease firing, for fear of hitting their own troops. Only the second line of trenches remains to be taken. From there the fire is intense. At the risk of revealing the emplacements of their machine-gun nests, the Germans are firing hysterically and incessantly, and it is practically impossible to raise your head. But the first line of trenches without the second would not be even half a victory, but barely one-tenth of it. Ordinary arithmetic is inapplicable in battle.

By seven o'clock our companies have fought their way through to the edge of the woods, eight hundred yards. Oak Grove has been captured. A few hundred dead Germans, eight prisoners, machine guns, automatics, rifles—the booty hasn't been counted yet, but it surely is considerable. There are some forty dugouts, partly abandoned and partly smashed. At their entrances, fragments of wood are mixed with snow blackened by exploded shells. Our ambulance men take away the wounded. Political Instructor Alexandrenko, commander of the storm groups, is carried on a stretcher by the commander of the regiment. He lies there mortally wounded, pale, gritting his teeth.

The entire grove is now ours, and the Germans begin to bombard it with trench mortars. It is dark now, and we can see pillars of snow and bursts of exploding shells among the trees. Our men, tired, breathing heavily, lie in the captured trenches. From sheer exhaustion many close their eyes, despite the deafening barrage. In the copse, near the edge of the woods, stooping and running in intervals between explosions, men are coming up with dinner for our soldiers in thermos containers. It is eight o'clock, a day of battle is drawing to its end. At divisional headquarters a report is being written, which, among other events, mentions the capture of Oak Grove.

(Western Front. April 16, 1942.)

A Man Who Came Back From There

✶✶

In four months of war I saw many horrors. I saw the mutilated bodies of children, the charred remnants of captured Red soldiers, villages razed to the ground, houses disemboweled by bombs. Yet the most horrible thing I encountered in this war is perhaps the candid and simple story of Machine Gunner Mikhail Ignatievich Kompaneets. It is the story of a week he passed in German captivity and of his escape.

It was an autumn night. A protective patrol to which Kompaneets belonged was moving to a new line. Their machine gun had been carried three hundred yards into the woods, when the soldiers noticed that one of the gunners was missing. Kompaneets left his group and went to look for the missing comrade.

He found him at the edge of the woods. Hit in the shoulder-blade by a stray bullet, he had fallen into a gully before he had time to call for help.

Kompaneets climbed down to him and, putting down his rifle, began to dress his wound. At that very moment, three German soldiers sneaked up unnoticed, jumped into the gully and fell upon Kompaneets who was leaning over his wounded comrade. The German soldiers led him away pushing him with the butts of their guns. As the four men were climbing up the slippery slope of the gully, Kompaneets drew his papers out of his pockets, pressed them in his hand and at an opportune moment threw them into the bushes.

A few minutes later they reached a German unit. A sergeant came out of a tent, silently rummaged in the prisoner's pockets, tore off his insignia with its Red Star and threw it to one side. None of the Germans spoke Russian. Then by order of the officer, one of the soldiers brought two shovels and with the help of gestures invited Kompaneets to dig a ditch. The German soldiers formed a circle around him in anticipation of the spectacle. The ditch was half dug, when a senior officer approached and said something in German. Apparently the show was to be postponed. The shovel was torn out of Kompaneets' hands, and he was led away. Two hours later he was taken to a railway station, where he found a group of about thirty other prisoners, almost all of them with at least one wound. A guard brought Kompaneets before a few officers in a little house. One of the officers spoke Russian. He asked the prisoner:

"Where are you from and where is your unit?"

Kompaneets said that if he had known the whereabouts of his unit he would not have been here. The officer did not continue questioning him; apparently he was to be cross-examined seriously at some other place.

A few unharmed and lightly wounded Red soldiers were then ordered to make stretchers for the rest. For about an hour they went about their task and having nailed together a few stretchers carried those of their comrades who were unable to walk to a covered truck parked on the road. The seriously wounded soldiers were placed in the truck first, but it soon became apparent that there would not be room for all the prisoners if some of them were left in a reclining position. The German officer ordered his subordinates to remove the wounded from the stretchers, and all the prisoners were jammed into the truck in a standing position. They drove away and after some time stopped for the night.

The wounded men asked to be carried out of the truck and placed on the ground. The Germans refused to comply with this wish, and every attempt to crawl out was met with the cold point of a bayonet. It was not until morning that the gravely wounded men were taken off the truck and put on the ground. Kompaneets did not know what their fate was; he never saw any of them again. The remaining prisoners were driven away. At noon they were led to a field kitchen where they received half a pound of bread and a cup of unsweetened tea.

Then in a little wood the Germans made three fires and three interpreters began to question the prisoners. The questioning took a long time; the Germans were particularly intent upon finding out whether there was not an officer among the captured Russians. A cold rain mixed with snow was falling. The interpreters stood near the fires warming their hands, but the prisoners were not allowed to come closer than ten steps to them.

After a few hours, the frozen and exhausted prisoners were drawn up in ranks of three and led farther on. At one point a tall officer wearing many crosses approached them. "Well, gentlemen," he said in Russian, "now your troubles are over. From now on you'll be protected from bullets and bombs and after the war you'll go home. Yes, yes, you'll be well off here. Only tell us, are there any commissioned or non-commissioned officers among you? We won't do them any harm, we only want to send them to another camp."

The prisoners remained silent. They were led on still further, and by night found themselves in a camp surrounded by barbed wire and a ditch. They were questioned again, each prisoner by three Germans simultaneously.

"One translated, another took notes, a third searched our pockets," Kompaneets explained.

[37]

At the end of the questioning he was asked what was his religion. "I thought, and thought, and said: 'Who the devil knows what my religion is?' That's what they wrote down. Then each of us got a string with a metal number tied around his neck and were forced to dip our thumbs into ink and leave our fingerprints on a sheet of paper. Then we were driven into low, damp mud huts without any food."

Thus began life in a concentration camp. Its main feature was organized, systematic starvation. It was a day-after-day torture, intended to drive the prisoners crazy, to turn them into animals. Every second day soup from horse meat was prepared in the camp. The horses were dressed in the camp where all the prisoners could see them. The meat was cut off and put aside. The Germans explained that it would be salted and used to feed the prisoners during the winter and that the bones were to be used for the soup.

Then the bones were thrown to the prisoners across the barbed wire. Crazed by hunger, the men avidly fell upon this food, while the German officers walked around with cameras and took pictures.

On the second or third day, the prisoners began to be taken out every morning to work on the road—digging ditches or dragging stones and wood. They were sent out in squads, some close to the camp, some further away. The squads who went far into the woods sometimes found carcasses of horses and remnants of food in abandoned trenches. Those who worked in the immediate vicinity of the camp were deprived of this "additional food." All the prisoners wanted to be assigned to one of the "privileged" squads. The Germans knew this and assigned to the distant sectors those prisoners who succeeded in getting out of camp first in the morning.

Thus every morning the prisoners rushed to the exit all together in a mad scramble to get out first. The German commandant enjoyed this spectacle and restored order by beating the men with his stick.

Sticks were an invariable piece of equipment for all the guards. In one hand they held a rifle, in the other a stick. All of them beat the prisoners. Some of them shouted and cursed, while others remained silent as they poked their gun butts into their victims' ribs. They beat the prisoners upon every possible pretext —for sticking their head out of the ranks, for raising their head too high, or dropping it too low—for anything.

One day a group of prisoners returning from work met a Finnish officer. He rushed at one of our men who had been walking a few inches out of ranks, beat him for a long time, finally tore his cap off and rummaging in his hair began to shout hysterically in Russian: "Perhaps you're a political instructor. Perhaps you have a sign on your skull." He accompanied these words with the most obscene curses.

Another day, a German who spoke Russian well visited the camp. He assembled the prisoners and affably suggested that they ask him any questions they wished to ask.

[39]

Someone asked naively: "How are things at the front?"

"At the front?" he said, "Well, Kandalaksha is surrounded and burning. Leningrad is burnt and half occupied."

"And how about Murmansk?"

"Murmansk, too, is burnt and surrounded," the officer replied glibly.

"Then why do you keep us here in the woods if everything is taken or surrounded?" asked one prisoner. "You should take us to some city, Murmansk or Kandalaksha, for instance."

"We would have done it but the roads are still occupied by the Reds at some places. And if we transfer you by sea, you might be sunk and then the Germans would be blamed for that, too."

"And why do you feed us so badly?"

"Well, soon we'll take everything we need, and you'll be better off."

Thus ended the "intimate talk."

By the middle of the second week of his imprisonment, Kompaneets realized that in a few more days he would be unable to move. Every third day the prisoners were given half a pound of bread, and every second day a bowl of soup. They were given water to drink only once a day. No salt was distributed. The men were rotting alive in their mud huts and sleeping on the bare ground.

The very first day Kompaneets began to think of escaping. He decided that he would take the first opportunity, that to postpone his escape would be dangerous. He found a comrade who wished to escape, too, Private Chepel.

Meanwhile the camp was moved to another spot. Two craters were dug in the ground and surrounded with barbed wire. In one of these craters, the prisoners slept; in the other, they were gathered, counted and formed into labor squads every morning, and counted again before being sent to sleep every evening. In this second crater there was a half-collapsed mud hut, which had been built during some work on the road.

One night, after roll call, Kompaneets and Chepel crawled into this mud hut and asked their comrades to cover them with earth and half-rotten planks.

After silence fell, the two men, half-dead from lack of air and dampness, waited for another two hours, until it was quite dark. Then they crawled out and entered the woods.

"Well, what's your plan?" said Chepel.

"My plan is simple," said Kompaneets. "For three days I have watched the Germans and I know in what direction they are least likely to go. We'll go that way, to the swamps."

Chepel hesitated for a minute.

"We'll die," he said gloomily. "We'll find our graves there."

"Never mind," said Kompaneets. "We've just gotten out of one grave, to get into another won't be so terrible."

The night was clear. For two hours they crawled through the swamp. Then they turned eastward, having got their bearings from the North Star. They walked for three days steering an eastward course by the sun and the stars. They crossed mountain torrents by wading or swimming, they froze almost to the point of losing consciousness during the cold northern nights.

On the second day they found two Finnish hand grenades in an abandoned trench. This made them feel more secure. At least they knew now that they would not return alive to the accursed camp. Twice they cut the black cables of German field telephones.

On the fourth day, Kompaneets and Chepel saw a frontier post amid a thick wood. They found it difficult to tell this part of their story, to relate their meeting with the frontier guards, their first words with a brother. They remembered that they wept, and then warmed themselves for a long time, in the Russian dugout.

And that's the whole story, simple and unsensational. No one gouged out Kompaneets' eyes, nor drove pins under his nails, and he did not see this being done to other prisoners. Possibly there was no expert torturer in his camp. Or perhaps the Germans did not intend to apply these methods in this case. They intended cold-bloodedly, systematically, to destroy the wounded who had the misfortune to be captured, to destroy them by cold and starvation, to destroy them quietly. . . .

Single Combat

✦✦✦

THE FOLLOWING TRUE STORY might also be called: "Fourteen against one." The fourteen were tanks— German medium tanks, Mark T-3, model 1939, each with a 50 mm. gun, two machine guns and a crew of four men. The one was a gun—a Russian 76 mm. gun, semi-automatic, with a crew of seven men commanded by Lieutenant Ilya Shuklin.

In these grim times, it is customary to begin the biography of a warrior with his first exploit. Ilya Shuklin's biography had just begun. If we were to tell of his "prehistoric" days, so to speak, it would be an ordinary story of a man born twenty years ago in the remote Altai village of Cherny Anud, a Russian schoolboy, who was first a Pioneer, then a Komsomol, first an organizer of childish games, then a passionate athlete. It would be one of a thousand stories which contain nothing remarkable up to the point when the old schoolteacher suddenly remembers a dishevelled little fellow who sat on a back bench and says with pride: "Yes, he was one of my pupils!"

Shuklin graduated from the tenth grade a few days after the opening of hostilities. The winter before he had often dreamed of finishing school as soon as possible. The music of artillery rang in his ears, two golden crossed guns on a black collar stirred his youthful imagination. His family had always loved artillery. Terenti Shuklin, his uncle, served in this branch of the army, and Andrei, his brother, was studying at artillery school. His best friend, Ivan Popugaev, was about to become an artillery lieutenant. In May, a few weeks before the war, Shuklin received letters from his friend and from his brother: "Try to get into the artillery, like us," wrote the boys who now considered themselves seasoned artillerymen.

On the first day of the war, Shuklin, returning home from a graduation test, sat down at his table and wrote an application beginning with the words: "I wish to enlist . . ."

His military training began. How long it seemed! What a torture it was to read communiqués from the front every day, and still be forced to go to the firing grounds and fire with training shells at practice targets! If it had been up to Shuklin, and if the students had been put through the course individually, he would have finished his training many days ahead of time.

It was a spring day, although the snow was not yet thawed. The train rolled across the snowy taiga, through countless Siberian stations, big and small, moving westward. In one of the cars sat a youthful lieutenant just graduated from school, with two brand new golden guns on a black collar. He was going to war. In a time of great ordeals, man has the noble right to feel himself indispensable to his native country, to feel that his personal presence is needed on the fields where the fate of his people is being decided in blood and fire. Not to go there would have been unbearable. Shuklin was going to the front with this sacred, youthful feeling in his heart. The thought of being idle was much more terrible to him than the thought of death.

At first he was assigned to a division occupying the second line of defense. This was almost war—but not really war. During the first days of July, the front moved closer to him. It was Shuklin's fate to receive his baptism of fire in difficult days. At the age of twenty, when you are full of romanticism and youthful enthusiasm, it is hard to begin your fighting experience with a retreat. It is true that Shuklin's division passed to furious counter-attacks several times a day and was always the last to retreat, fighting its way through the enemy encirclement and destroying German tanks, but retreat is still retreat, and during

[45]

those days Shuklin suffered as never before in his life.

He managed to save his guns and his men except for a few who fell on the field of battle before his eyes. In those days he fought much and fiercely, but he still had no feeling of accomplishing anything, of doing the things he had dreamed of at school and had aspired to do when leaving for the front.

In the second half of July, Shuklin's division stopped retreating, and soon began to attack. Life somehow grew more bearable at once. During the retreat, Shuklin had felt only hatred and anger; now for the first time he knew the rapture of battle. And passing the places at which he had fired he could at last see the results of his work with his own eyes. Before, in the short minutes of respite between battles, he had silently closed his eyes and fallen asleep instantaneously as though falling into a bottomless abyss; now, however tired he might be, he felt the need of discussing the day's battle, the suddenly remembered details. And he noticed that his men shared these feelings. For the first time in the war, gathering together at night, they sang songs, and his gun commander, Akinshin, the life of the group, imitated musical instruments with his voice.

Shuklin's guns worked a great deal, harder than ever before, and once specialists sent from the field workshop came just before nightfall and declared that it would be dangerous, or, more exactly, impossible, to continue using these guns. The divisional commander gave orders to remove them to a grove behind the next village, for overhauling.

All night and all morning the guns remained in the workshop. By noon the sounds of an increasingly fierce barrage were heard coming from the advance positions. The regimental commander's aide galloped up and, without dismounting from his foaming horse, asked what the condition of the guns was and whether they could be put to use at once. The workmen told him that only one gun was fit for firing, and even this, they added, shaking their heads, might explode.

"Never mind!" cried Akinshin, the gun commander, suddenly jumping up from his place. "I know my gun, it won't explode! Let's go, Comrade Lieutenant!" But Shuklin did not have to be told this. He had already given the order to move up to the firing positions. The regimental commander's aide explained that a group of German tanks were counter-attacking in an effort to stop our advance, and that for the moment this was the only gun at his disposal.

The gun was hitched to a tractor, and the tractor rushed forward. Shuklin had galloped away without waiting for his gun, to choose a suitable position. Lieutenant Maltsev, the platoon commander, went with him. Shuklin chose a position situated in a field of thick rye, on the crest of a hill which offered a good view of the crest of a neighboring hill where the German tanks were expected to appear.

Shuklin waited impatiently for his gun. At last it

[47]

moved up with a tractor loaded with shells. The lieutenant set up his gun and once again rode up to the very top of the hill. At that very moment he saw on the horizon the silhouettes of the German tanks moving toward a village on the left. First he saw ten tanks, then more and more. Altogether he counted thirty of them. One after the other they emerged on the crest of the neighboring hill. This was a clearly visible spot, situated exactly at the crossing of the roads marked on the staff map. Shuklin checked the position of this spot on the map, determined his distance from it and set a tank afire with his very first shell.

The tanks were attacking him headlong, outflanking the hill. Shuklin's first shell was followed by a number of others. Mounted on his horse twenty yards from the gun, he corrected the range and repeatedly gave the order: "Fire." After three German tanks were put out of action, the other tank crews discovered the position of the gun and opened fire at it. Shells began to explode all around. By Shuklin's order, the gun immediately changed position. Having lost a few more tanks, the Germans again found the range of Shuklin's gun, and their shells again began to explode close to it.

Shuklin continued correcting the range from his horse. The rye was tall and he had to remain on horseback to have a clear view of the battlefield. After the tenth German tank had been crippled, the Russians began to run short of shells. Shuklin sent Osadchev,

the tractor driver, to bring up more shells from the
rear. The tractor went straight across the open field.
All around shell fragments were flying, but Shuklin
could see his machine moving toward its destination,
and he knew that its driver was alive. Meanwhile he
kept firing his gun. Lieutenant Maltsev and Gunner
Romashev were wounded by shell fragments, and
Red Soldier Kaiumov replaced the latter at the sight.
The tractor returned with a supply of shells just in
time. Osadchev with the aid of Liaison Man Lon-
chakov, began to help loading, but at that moment
he, too, was wounded in the side.

Twelve German tanks were now burning in front
of the gun crew. The others began to retreat behind
the hill, except two, which occupied the crest and
opened fire, this time from fixed positions. Shuklin
again was faced with the necessity of moving his gun,
but the wounded driver lay motionless in the rye. For
the first time in this battle Shuklin dismounted from
his horse, hitched the gun to the tractor, and drove it
a distance of fifty yards. At that moment a liaison
man came galloping up from divisional headquarters.

"Who is firing from here?" he asked abruptly.

"I," said Shuklin in a tired voice as he got off the
tractor.

"The divisional commander asked me to convey his
thanks," cried the liaison man.

Again Shuklin mounted his horse, and again shots
resounded. A few hits, and two more German tanks
were put out of action. The last tank, the fourteenth,

received a particularly lucky hit, and it broke into flames at once.

A minute's pause followed. Then, from behind the hill, moving straight across the rye, emerged five German trucks full of infantry. They made a detour around the ravine and steered straight at the gun. Shuklin hurled a few shells at them which proved too short, and then ordered Akinshin to transfer his fire farther back toward the edge of the ravine.

The Germans, frightened by the first shell, deployed and stopped near the edge of the ravine. There they were hit by a succession of shells. Only two cars succeeded in moving down the ravine. The three others received direct hits and took fire. The shot that set the third German truck ablaze was the last to be fired by Shuklin's gun. The mechanics' warning proved partly justified: the gun-lock had stopped functioning. But from the grove behind it new guns appeared at last.

The fourteen German tanks put out of action and burned were clearly visible on their hill. Some were still smoking, and others were just motionless black spots in the rye.

The artillerymen were preparing a soup made of young potatoes. A tasty smoke rose above the field kettles. German long range guns were firing at the grove, and above the fresh shell craters a bluish powder smoke was also rising. I sat beside Shuklin. He had mischievous black eyes and a gay youthful face, which grew suddenly virile and serious as he told of the battle. His dictionary did not contain the word "exploit." Possibly he did not consider what he had done today an exploit, but from the happy expression in his eyes it was evident that this battle had fulfilled his deepest, most ardent desires. He remembered why he had come here, and his face was radiant.

Then, after thinking for a while, he began to speak of things which had no relation to the war—his life with his father and mother who were now in the distant town of Oirot-Tura; his comrades from the same town where he had been a member of the Komsomols, his girl, Valia Nekrasova, who had gone to the Far East to join the navy, and who had written to him on her way there, from Novosibirsk. And as I listened to him I wanted his father and mother, when they read my dispatch, to feel proud of their son, and the Komsomols of Oirot-Tura to remember their comrade, and Valia Nekrasova to know that she was loved by a really fine man with the level eyes and strong hands of a soldier.

Reconnaissance Behind the Lines

✶✶

FOR FIVE DAYS the north wind from the Barents Sea had swept over the roads of Finland. A wet autumn blizzard lashed the window panes. At the edge of the town, in a small frame house in a hermetically sealed room, the men who had just returned from out there were gathered around the supper table. Only yesterday they had journeyed many miles from here, through the forests and mountains of Finland. Now they were sitting under electric lights, with a white table-cloth such as they had not seen for a long time in front of them. Their commander offered three toasts one after the other. The first to the leader of our country, the second to the long-range scouts, those who had just returned and were now sitting here and to their comrades who had left and were now wandering in Finland, and a third for those who had not come back and never would come back from this campaign, who had sold their lives dearly, resisting to the last cartridge, to the last hand grenade, to the last breath.

It is hard to write about these men, these long-range scouts. Their exploits are silent. Their paths are unknown. Only the mute bodies of their killed enemies can testify for them. Imagine furious gales, wind and snow, fog descending over the hills, short nights spent without fires and weekly trips across the mountains. Open a map of northern Finland and point at random at the long Finnish names of the mountains, rivers and ravines. And you will almost never be wrong; yes, they have been there. Our long-range scouts walked there or crawled there and they know these regions a thousand times better than the German chasseurs and Alpine riflemen who arrogantly display bronze armbands with the inscription "For Narvik." The Germans intended to earn a second armband up here in the North, "For Murmansk." Instead they won stakes topped with helmets which were driven with difficulty into this stony soil.

Beside me in Murmansk, toward which the Germans had vainly been trying to advance for three months, sat Lieutenant Karpov. Thanks to him, a few dozen German graves had recently been added to the northland.

Only a few days before the lieutenant had taken six

[53]

men with him for a certain operation—six, he did not want any more, only six men in each of whom he trusted as in himself. Only those who have had experience in reconnaissance know how important this is. All night their boat sailed over the sea. A storm was raging. Amid furiously rolling waves, in utter darkness, the boat reached the shore, passing an enemy battery. All day long hidden in the fjords, our scouts observed the movements of the German patrols and decided at which spot they would cross the front lines. That night, when dusk fell in the woods, near a great waterfall which rushed over the rocks all the way down to the bay, they said goodbye to the commander of the rifle platoon, who had accompanied them—thus far the last Soviet citizen they saw on the edge of the enemy's territory. They exchanged a brief handshake, then he vanished.

They walked in pairs, so that a sudden volley of machine guns would not wipe them all out at once. Every time they stumbled, stones clattered down the slopes. Every little move they made might become a question of life and death. One of the scouts had forgotten to take the iron clamps off his heels. As a result he now had to move over the stones practically on all fours. When his heel hit a stone, sparks flew out which could be seen miles away in the dark night. The road along the ravine was mined. The scouts had to crawl along the side of the road, on the narrow, slippery, stone-covered bridge.

There the Germans heard them for the first time.

Somewhere to the left of them a rocket rose obliquely in the sky and burned for thirty seconds. During these long seconds our scouts lay on an open ridge, pressed against the stones, motionless as the earth itself. Just as they managed to roll noiselessly down the slope, a second rocket went up exactly above the spot where they had been lying. The third and fourth rockets rose further away from them. Next to them on the other side of the road, was a cliff. The moon rose, and in its light the silhouette of the German sentry on top of it could be clearly seen from below. To cock one's rifle and remove him would have been a matter of seconds. But caution above all! The scouts advanced noiselessly in the shadow of the cliff. Behind the cliff was a lake. The moon was shining on their right, and in order to prevent their shadows from falling on the smooth surface of the lake, they climbed laboriously over the stones and took a detour to the left. To one side, they could hear the neighing of horses, the clattering of pans in field kitchens and even the conversations of the Germans.

The scouts moved forward doggedly. At last, the first two stopped; in front of them loomed a row of cliffs. The second, main line of the German positions passed along the ledges of these cliffs. In front of them were the observation posts and machine-gun nests; behind them, in rocky excavations, the big dugouts where the garrison took shelter at night. The scouts crawled along the fissures, inky black in their double shadows. Now they were ten yards from the dugouts. They could hear the Germans talking; they saw the light of the cigarette in the mouth of a sentry patrolling near the dugout. He was walking back and forth nervously puffing at his cigarette and from time to time directing his flashlight at the rocks. The scouts lay flat on the ground. Several times a strip of light passed over a stone no more than half a yard away from their eyes. Gradually the voices of the Germans grew silent. A few more minutes, and the scouts could have begun their task. But one of them made a false move, and the muzzle of his automatic hit a stone making a barely perceptible sound. The German sentry turned around abruptly.

"Who goes there?" he asked in a loud voice.

Then, as though frightened by the sound of his own voice, he repeated the question twice in a low tone, and directed his flashlight toward the scouts. But before the beam of light had reached them, the lieutenant fired a short burst with his automatic. The sentry fell. Seven shadows rose from under the cliff and rushed to the entrances of the dugouts. One after the other, into the black holes of the dugouts, flew hand grenades. In the light of their explosions flying planks of wood and stones could be seen. In one of the dugouts something took fire. Screaming men jumped out of them and fell to the ground. The scouts calmly fired short volleys at them from the shadows. Then a second of silence followed. Now nobody jumped out any more.

As they approached the silent dugouts, the scouts

hurled a few more hand grenades into them. From the nearby hilltops German machine guns hurriedly turned upon the dugouts, began to fire. A few minutes later they were joined by minethrowers. Another minute, and somewhere from the rear came the first roar of artillery.

It was time to leave. But how? By the path below, along the valley, the same one by which they had come? The lieutenant decided otherwise. He led his men by another path, farther up. They climbed higher and higher along steep and rocky slopes, and as they came to the top of the ridge they saw that along the path of their supposed retreat German mines were uselessly exploding, one after another. Apparently, the Germans had decided that we had occupied the hilltop and the dugouts, and they peppered it with mines and shells. Not one inch of it was left unscathed. The Germans who had survived the raid of our scouts were now being killed by their own mines and shells. Still our scouts continued to advance.

The first dim lights of the dawn were seen. Now along the ten miles of the German line not one man slept. Machine gunners fired at every rustle, every sound. Less and less time remained before sunrise. To shorten their route the scouts had to cut across wide ravines, under enemy fire. Sergeant Volosheniuk was wounded first. He did not say anything to his comrades, but clenching his teeth continued to move forward painfully dragging his wounded leg. It was now almost daylight. Only a short stretch remained to the shore, when a machine-gun volley from above killed Sergeant Kozlovski and wounded Volosheniuk a second time in the same leg. Now he could no longer walk. His comrades rushed to help him. But a new burst of fire wounded two more of the group: Khrabrin in the chest, and the lieutenant himself in one hand, one leg and the face. The scouts lay flat on the ground. The lieutenant crawled to Kozlovski and turned his face upward. He was dead, he could no longer be helped.

Finally the enemy fire stopped. The scouts covered Kozlovski's body with stones and branches. Then they crawled on, supporting Volosheniuk who was exhausted from his wounds. It was too late to make a detour, the only possible course was to break through along the shore. Fortunately for our men, the tide was going out, uncovering sandbars and small islets. Helping their bleeding comrades, the scouts waded knee-deep in water along the shore, hiding behind the stony little islets. They stumbled cautiously over the slippery, seaweed-covered stones. They reached our positions late in the morning. The three unharmed men supported their three wounded comrades. One had remained forever on the rocks of Finland, his motionless hands folded over his chest. And far behind the front lines the artillery still thundered. German guns and minethrowers were still firing on the stony hilltop presumably occupied by those elusive Russians and now the grave of several dozen German soldiers.

This was a one-night operation, brief and sudden. But all the men who sat beside me at the table had been in many other such dangerous affairs. They had been on expeditions lasting two weeks during which they had never once made a fire, never once boiled water, never had a hot meal. They had crossed swamps at night wading in water up to their knees, and hidden in quagmires for whole days, waiting for an opportunity to strike. They had advanced until they reached their objective, subsisting on the un- salted and over-fresh meat of a deer they happened to encounter. Seventy miles behind the German lines, almost under the very noses of the Nazis, they had made dents in their daggers and used them to saw off telegraph and telephone lines. They had cut down the posts and destroyed the cables with stones. They had managed to take prisoners and bring them back to our lines by secret paths. They had reached the enemy shores in tiny skiffs across the stormy Barents Sea and swum to the cliffs through the icy water. After completing a raid and inflicting losses on the enemy, after braving mortal dangers, they had waited patiently in little hidden bays for good weather which would permit our ships to rescue them. They had disciplined themselves till each of them was worth ten men, unflinching, fearless, unsparing of their lives, and ruthless toward the enemy.

Now they sat here, around the table, celebrating

the end of yesterday's expedition and preparing for tomorrow's. And over there, beyond the front line, from the left to the right flanks, rockets soared incessantly over the German positions; as soon as one went out another blazed up. Our scouts have taught the Germans to fear the night. Searchlights, electric lamps, rockets which might attract our planes, seem preferable to them to silent death at the hands of our scouts, to the darkness of the impenetrable northern night during which, for months now, no German soldier has been able to find sleep or rest.

Daring

✶✶

IN A LITTLE BAY, almost invisible against the background of the brown, spotty, snow-covered cliffs, gray torpedo boats huddled close to the shore. The early northern dusk was descending on the Barents Sea; soon it would be night, the best time for the work of these craft.

The weather report was discouraging, and the echoes of the storm raging out to sea rolled in even here in the bay. But the captain, Senior Lieutenant Mol, had not lost hope of going out hunting at sea tonight.

"They can swim like ducks," he said, pointing affectionately at a torpedo boat which was swaying near the shore. "And then, if you take the weather too seriously here in the north, it won't be long before you're a landlubber. To be sure there's a saying you must always be very polite with the Barents Sea, but we sometimes treat it like an old chum, and everything is fine, believe it or not, even in such eggshells as mine."

While watching for the darkness, Mol told us of a few cases in which he had treated the Barents Sea "like an old chum," and everything, as he said, was nevertheless "fine."

A short time ago the Germans had decided to send a convoy from Norway to Finland, relying upon a stormy sea which their big ships could easily manage but which, they thought, would prevent our torpedo boats from sailing. Mol was ordered out to sea. He sailed before nightfall. The eastern sky was already dark, but the west, where the sun had just set, was still illumined by a red glow to the horizon. Against this glow Mol saw the silhouettes of the German transports some distance away. They moved along the horizon, and it seemed that the light was moving parallel to them.

Gaining speed, one torpedo boat by now in almost complete darkness, approached the promontory near which begins the deep and jagged bay of Finland. Hugging the shore, its motor making slow, almost silent turns, the torpedo boat entered the bay. Advancing in the inky-black shadow of the steep rocky shore, it turned each cliff. The very boldness of this maneuver to some extent insured its success. The

Germans did not expect torpedo boats to come so near the shore, so that their patrol ships were cruising much further out to sea.

Here the torpedo boat was perhaps protected by the cliff from the fire of the shore batteries, but it was threatened by another danger: a machine gun hidden among the cliffs near the water could easily put the boat out of action.

In complete darkness the torpedo boats went far up the bay and huddled close to the shore at the very spot where, according to the captain's calculations, the German batteries were emplaced high above it, but too near to hit it. Here the captain waited, knowing that the convoy would not expect to be attacked from the direction of its own shore, under the nose of its own batteries.

An hour later the transports appeared. Our torpedo boats let a small escort vessel pass undisturbed; then, seeing the silhouettes of a destroyer and a large transport behind it, they moved away from the shore and deploying with lightning speed, launched a salvo of torpedoes against both ships. Deafening explosions rang out in the narrow bay, resounding from the mountains which ringed it on three sides. The echoes were still thundering when the German ships began to sink. The moment the explosions occurred, huge sheaves of fire lit up the bay. The shore batteries fired tracer shells, the undamaged ships unleashed all their guns, machine guns from escort vessels and from the shore rattled without interruption. "In brief," Mol commented, "we were received with triumphal fireworks which made me think of the Park of Culture and Rest."

Now our torpedo boats no longer needed to conceal their presence. At full speed they roared out of the bay.

A few days later our command decided to repeat the operation. Once again we relied on the boldness of our maneuver; the Germans would hardly expect us to repeat our raid so soon and with identical tactics. Once again, having left shortly before sunset, our torpedo boats sailed at night along the ragged coastline, searching each bay. But they found no Germans.

Daybreak was approaching. We knew with certainty that somewhere in the fjords German ships were hiding on their way to or from Norway. Mol decided that in the daylight the Germans would not leave the bay nearest to us, but that they might venture to sail in waters where they would not have to fear our long-range shore batteries. He gave orders to steer a westward course, toward the shores of Norway.

An hour later the sun began to rise. By then our torpedo boats had reached one of the little fjords and hid in the shadow of a cliff. The tenacity of our men was rewarded. A few minutes later two unescorted German transports going full speed emerged from behind the cliff. A brief command, and the motors roared. A salvo of torpedoes launched from a short distance finished one ship. Fifteen seconds later, the other went down. Plunging into the waves, the torpedo boats hurried away. It was now so light their little silhouettes could be easily distinguished on the surface of the sea. But the Germans directed searchlights on them and their shore batteries opened fire. Two pillars of black smoke was all that remained of the German transport.

"Rapidity, surprise, daring, are all that is needed for success," said Mol, as he concluded the story of these sinkings. "And one thing more: a stout Russian heart, the kind every one of my boys has."

Outfighting the Fighter Planes

✦✦

THIS CALM MAN had practised many trades, perhaps too many, in his thirty years of life. And each one had left its mark on him. He had been a *besprizorni*, then a shepherd, then a glass-blower; then he had joined the air force, and there, too, had tried out several "trades"—he was by turns a scout, a bombardier, and finally the pilot of a fighter plane. He had flown over many parts of this world, and the four thousand and more flights he had to his credit before the war proved extremely useful to him now. He was accustomed to fly under any conditions, and he had learned, once he had flown over a place, to remember it forever.

Now Senior Lieutenant Kovalenko—for that was his

name—had turned up here, on the far northern front. There was no time to have a look around and to get accustomed to things. Air battles began the very first day. He had to fly, and to fly well.

"In those first days they had more machines than we had. Our only salvation was to fly and fight better than they did," Kovalenko said, recalling his first air battles on the northern front.

The air over this country is just as bad as its climate. Only rarely was it possible to keep a straight course during a flight. To fight the enemy, to sneak up upon him and take him by surprise, it was necessary to fly cautiously, maneuvering along winding mountain gullies. The game of hide-and-seek, aerial ambushes, eternal watchfulness—Kovalenko had to turn all these stern laws of northern warfare against the enemy.

The term "landmark" has only a relative meaning in this country. Hundreds of snow-bound gullies and cliffs passed under the wings of the plane, as like each other as two drops of water, and one needed a sharp, practised eye to distinguish the cliff which was to serve as a landmark in a given square. This was no easy task. It was no wonder that the commander of one of the German bombing planes, Lieutenant Schuppius, who was ordered to fly from Stettin to Kirkenes, actually landed eight miles from Kandalaksha. Kovalenko recalled this incident with a smile —he could still see the face the German made when told where he was.

To talk with Kovalenko was difficult and easy at the same time. It was easy because everything he said was accurate, well thought out, verified. He spoke slowly, as though he were watching the incident he related unfold before his mind's eye. And if he forgot anything, even a detail, he stopped and did not continue until he recalled that detail, too. But it was difficult to talk to him, because he did not like to talk about himself. No, it was not that he was excessively modest—although he was really modest, and his superior officer credited him with a much higher number of planes shot down than the number he mentioned himself. The cause of his reticence was his philosophy of air warfare, not his modesty. His attitude was typical of Soviet flyers, it expressed all their tactical conceptions. What was important for Kovalenko was not the number of planes he himself shot down, but the general result of the battle, the achievements of the entire flight participating in it.

"We have many young flyers in our squadron, and from the very first day we made them understand what it meant to come to a comrade's aid during a battle, and how much more important the general result of a battle was than one's personal exploit," said Kovalenko. And it was no accident that when asked to relate his most successful encounters with the enemy, he spoke not of those battles in which he himself shot down the largest number of planes, but of those which in his opinion were remarkable from the point of view of tactical coordination.

"One day," he reminisced, "Semenenko and I cut into a swarm of Messerschmidts. I hit one German, but seeing that a Messerschmidt was on Semenenko's tail I let go my German and went to help Semenenko, whose adversary, taken by surprise, was quickly shot down. Having got rid of him, the two of us managed to catch up with and finish my own German whom I had to let go a minute before."

The following day a similar incident took place, but this time the roles of the two Russian pilots were reversed. Kovalenko engaged a Messerschmidt, but before he had had time to shoot it down, two others appeared on his tail. Semenenko attacked them from the rear, shot one down and forced the other to turn aside. Then Kovalenko, whose tail was now protected by his friend, finished the Messerschmidt he had taken up at the beginning of the engagement.

Kovalenko told us how he was helped by his knowledge of the country, by his willingness to continue the battle under any conditions, to engage the enemy in gullies, maneuvering amidst cliffs, and sometimes descending almost to the ground.

"I recall one case," he said, smiling, "in which we fighters bombed German positions with German help. Yes, yes, we actually bombed them.

"The sky was full of clouds, snow was falling, the mountain tops were invisible. Seven of our planes were flying over our positions on the way to a strafing expedition, when we suddenly noticed bombs bursting below us. Bombs usually fall from above, so we at once looked up—where were they dropping from? Above us was a whole squadron of bombers and fighters. In a first attack, Safanov and I each shot down one bomber. Circling around the enemy planes and attacking them from all sides, we drove them back toward their own positions. Another bombing plane took fire. Then, unable to stand it any longer, the others began to get rid of their bombs by dropping them on their own positions. I got somewhat excited and found myself amid such a swarm of German planes that my prime concern was to avoid a collision and wriggle out of the crowd. Nor did the Germans have an easy time of it, they were crowding me so from all sides that they could not fire at me for fear of hitting one of their own planes. Finally, I managed to find a hole and dived down to join my squadron. This time we performed a double assignment, so to speak, we bombed the Germans with their own planes.

"But I prefer fighters to bombers, it's more fun to shoot them down. I love the 110, it's a good machine, I mean it's big, it's a good target and it has a lot of firepower, it's not afraid to attack head-on. That's what we like. I always meet the first onslaught headlong and fly right at the enemy. Usually he turns around at the last minute, relying on the machine gunner in his tail. While he makes this turn, I concentrate my fire on his tail, and usually get him," Kovalenko concluded calmly.

He told me all this without a smile, in the business-like tone of a professional, a master of his trade. You felt that he really loved "Mr. 110," as he called the Messerschmidt 110, that he loved it because it is a strong machine, and attacks head-on more frequently than "Mr. 109."

He sat at the entrance to the dugout, pensively tapping his boot on the snow, a squatty little man with bright eyes and a dull voice. Now he was in full kit with his helmet and parachute. But he was always calm, alert, on his guard, not only now, but also when he sat at table without his battle equipment. It was as though he were always in full kit wherever he found himself.

"Kovalenko?" said the wing commander. "Oh, Kovalenko's a good flyer. Last month he shot down about ten planes."

"He says seven," I observed.

"Seven? Well, let it be seven if he insists. Incidentally, all his victims are fighters. We call him here the 'fighter of fighters.'"

Hearing this nickname, involuntarily I evoked Kovalenko's strong, heavy-set figure, his dull voice, which at some moments undoubtedly becomes imperious and stern, and once again his calm words rang in my ears: "I love the 110, it's a good machine, it has a lot of firepower, it's not afraid to attack head-on. . . ."

On the Road to Petsamo

✦✦✦

THE GERMANS NEVER LEARNED how our men got behind their lines. From the sea? But that night and the night before a furious gale had swept the Barents Sea. From the air? But for the last three days the skies had been covered by a dense snowy blanket. By land, across the German positions? But these were guarded by patrols along the entire front, and for the last three nights not a shot had been fired there. In brief, the Germans did not know, and they do not know to this day how a company of frontier guards slipped through their lines and wreaked havoc from the coast to the Petsamo road. And as the Germans do not know it, we shall not try to find out either. After all, that is what frontier guards are for—to pass over the frontier.

Well, by one means or another, one hundred and fifty frontier guards and twenty sappers turned up one night at 10:00 P.M. deep behind the German lines, in snowbound crevices among the cliffs, only a few miles away from the highway connecting Petsamo with the front.

Snow was falling. The advance scouts moving with extreme difficulty through deep drifts climbed up to a cliff from which the road could be seen. For three hours they lay motionless on this bare cliff, lashed by fierce blasts of wind, keeping their numb fingers warm with the greatest difficulty. This sector extended almost to the frontier, and they knew the terrain as well as they knew their own names.

The night was dark and foggy. Endless lines of crags made it difficult for them to orientate themselves, but they had to be on the road at an appointed place and hour. They could not afford to make a mistake of half an hour or a quarter of a mile—everything depended on that. In the impenetrable darkness the scouts were to destroy an enemy bridge—this was the object of their expedition.

The Germans helped them. At one point on the road they slowed up their cars. The headlights would stop moving for a second, and patches of light would fall on the road. Sharp eyes could discern part of the railing and the pavement of the bridge lifted out of the darkness for an instant. Then the cars continued. The scouts reported that they had located their objective, and by 1:00 A.M. the entire detachment was with them,

[73]

hugging the cliff, only half a mile from the road. The commissar and the commander divided the effectives. Political Instructor Senkin, Lieutenant Egunov and Sapper Lebedev were sent to the bridge; Lieutenant Yakushev, to the mud huts near the bridge; Lieutenant Sorokolad to the road, to cut off the cars moving toward the bridge. The rest were left behind; after the completion of the operation they were to cover the retreat and receive the blows of the pursuing enemy.

Noiselessly the orders were passed from man to man. Four groups, silent and almost invisible in their white cloaks, slipped down the snowy slope. A minute later no one remained on the cliff.

Political Instructor Senkin, Lieutenant Egunov and Sapper Lebedev were all extremely cool-headed men. That was why they were sent with the group going to the bridge. Everything depended on their coolness. They were not to open fire before reaching the bridge. But what if they encountered sentries, or cars, or dugouts? That was their business—whether they encountered obstacles or not, they must not fire a shot before reaching a point fifty yards from the bridge. They were answerable with their lives for carrying out this order.

Senkin was in command. Five hundred yards from the bridge they ran into a mud hut. Noiselessly detaching a part of his group he left several soldiers at the entrance, ordering them to lie quietly and await the first shot. The others moved ahead.

Two hundred yards from the bridge, three little houses stood at the side of the road. Another group detached itself noiselessly and crawled toward the houses. The others continued to advance upon the bridge. Up the hills and in the gullies. The frontier guards helped the sappers carry their heavy boxes of precious T.N.T.

Only fifty yards now separated them from the bridge. The black silhouettes of the sentries could be seen when Sergeant Gudkov, who was first in line, ran into a trench dug at the very entrance to the bridge. From behind a hillock a German leaped out: "Halt!"

Gudkov stooped and fired from his knees. The German, too. Both missed. Tracer bullets passed over Gudkov's head. He took up a hand grenade and hurled it at the German. Then he ran a few steps, hurled two more hand grenades into the open door of one mud hut and advanced further toward the bridge.

Frontier Guard Evseev leaped to a second mud hut and tore open the door. It was packed full of people. Evseev wanted to hurl a hand grenade, but it got stuck in his belt. He slammed the door, held it closed with his knees for a second, unhooked his hand grenade and, reopening the door, hurled the missile into a pile of shouting Germans who were firing in disorder. Then he ran toward the bridge, firing as he ran. His magazine was soon emptied; Evseev took it out and was about to put in a new one when two sentries jumped upon him close to the bridge. Again a frightened, hysterical "Halt!" and shots. Evseev hurled the empty magazine with a shout of "hand grenade!" The German sentries dropped flat onto the ground. Evseev

[75]

used this second for putting the new magazine in his tommy gun, and when the sentries got up he liquidated them with one burst and rushed to the bridge.

By the light of the shots two other sentries were seen running over the bridge. A short rattle, and one of them spread out his hands and, staggering against the railing, fell into the black water.

The way to the bridge was open.

"Sappers, on the bridge!" ordered Lieutenant Lebedev, and six sappers ran to the first span amidst the whistling of bullets. There was disorderly shooting from all sides. From behind came the sound of exploding hand grenades—the mud huts were being blown up. From the other bank of the river, German tommy gunners kept up a barrage of tracer bullets. The sappers huddling close to the pavement began to tie their explosives to the bridge with clumsy, frostbitten fingers. The frontier guards took up positions behind the rocks near the bridge and, with their automatics, shot down every German who showed himself. They had to hold out for five minutes at any price. During these five long minutes, the sappers, in spite of their frozen fingers, would attach the explosives, light the fuse and blow up at least one span of the bridge.

From behind came the sounds of new explosions. It was Sorokolad and Yakushev smashing up mud huts and burning cars further down the road. Explosions followed closely upon one another, but the most important one—a nearby deafening explosion—had not yet come.

And suddenly, even before the sound reached our ears, the world seemed to shake, struck with a powerful blast of air. A deafening roar, a short red burst, and then a dense black pillar of smoke visible even on the background of that black sky.

"It's done!" cried a sapper bending close to Political Instructor Senkin's ear. "The bridge is blown up!" and taking a handful of snow he wiped his burning, sweating face.

Our men began to retreat from the bridge, fighting their way with hand grenades, blowing up the remaining mud huts as they passed them. To the right, on the road, machine guns continued rattling, and explosions rent the air. The second and third groups had apparently not yet finished their task.

In fact, a battle was still raging. When Yakushev and Sorokolad at the head of their detachments reached the edge of the woods, they found a group of Germans in a glade near the road. Dressed in dark overcoats, shivering with cold, and stamping their feet, they were smoking and talking. The frontier guards waited. As yet no sound had come from the bridge on their left. The Germans were so close that they could almost touch them with their hands. First the bridge and then it would be their turn, the supreme moment for those who now warmed themselves and conversed for the last time.

Finally a shot resounded from the left. This was the shot fired by Sergeant Gudkov from his knees when he was discovered by the sentry. When they heard this shot, the Germans in the glade began to rush about in all directions. Sorokolad and Yakushev threw their frontier guards into the fray. The first hand grenade flew at the Nazi mob, killing ten on the spot. The others took to flight. The frontier guards pursued them and found themselves on the road.

Then a shot came from behind. Yakushev looked back. Between the road and the bushes, deeply buried in the ground to serve as dugouts, stood a group of trailers. Our men had not noticed them before; now the light in their windows and the cracks in their doors were clearly visible. Turning his platoon around, Yakushev rushed to the German dugouts. Hand grenades flew into the windows of the trailers.

Now there was great agitation among the Germans; some shots were fired. Corporal Bogachev climbed up onto the roof of the biggest dugout, trying to drop a hand grenade into the chimney. But the chimney was tall and slanted to one side. Putting his arm around it Bogachev pulled it out, and threw two hand grenades into the hole. The explosion blew up the entire structure, and hurled Bogachev from the roof. He had one hand grenade left. He ran up to the next structure, looked through a crack in the door and saw a German officer standing with a kerosene lamp in one hand and a pistol in the other. Bogachev tore the door off its hinges and hurled his hand grenade inside. The officer fell and a flaming jet of kerosene crept along the floor.

Shots were still being fired from some of the mud huts. The frontier guards hurled bombs into the chimneys or, tearing off the roofing of planks or tarred paper, fired inside with their tommy guns. Then one enthusiastic soldier shouted, "Hurrah!" The remaining mud huts were stormed. The night was rent by the roar of explosions and the crash of broken doors. Sorokolad's platoon, smashing several cars as they ran, also rushed upon the mud huts.

Individual Germans kept jumping out, but the frontier guards concealed in the bushes clearly saw them in the light of the fires and shot them down one by one. The Germans fell, spreading their arms out grotesquely. Many of them wore only their underwear and helmets. One, who had apparently learned a few Russian words somewhere on the plundered fields of the Ukraine, shouted in a voice that broke at every word: "Russ, Russ, no shoot! What you doing?! You mustn't!" There was panicky fear in his cry, but it did not arouse pity in any of the frontier guards. They kept on coolly shooting down the Germans, who were at last getting their deserts. This was not a real revenge—it was only the beginning of it.

Germans were being shot down everywhere—in doorways and in windows, on the white snow of the glade, in automobiles and in trucks. Cars were being blown up with bombs, and motors blasted with armor-piercing bullets. In all this noise and din, our men almost missed the explosions that resounded to the left of the bridge, and which were the signal for them to start the retreat.

Keeping up their fire, they began quickly to march

away from the road into the woods and ravines. The machine gunners now bore the brunt of the action. Concealed behind rocks near the road they covered our departure. The last man to leave was Machine Gunner Tronin, who continued firing until all his comrades had gone; then he followed them. Suddenly from a mud hut which he had not noticed before, four automatics began to fire simultaneously. Spreading wide his legs, Tronin lay down comfortably near the small northern birch and opened fire. From the trajectory of their bullets he knew the position of the German automatic riflemen. The frontier guards who had taken over for a while now continued to retreat, protected by their machine gun. To save his cartridges Tronin fired short bursts. The four automatics, having felt out his position, opened a furious fire. Over Tronin's head all the branches of the little birch trees were blown off and fell on his back. He decided to play dead. He stuck his head into the snow putting a hand grenade at his side.

A minute went by. There was silence. Suddenly forty yards away from him the door of the mud hut opened. Two Germans clearly visible by the light of the lamp burning inside peeped out. Tronin gave a long burst with his machine gun and the two Germans fell. Two others slammed the door from the inside and re-opened fire. Then Tronin crawled away from his machine gun, toward the mud hut. The Germans were still firing in the direction of the machine gun, when Tronin, having climbed up on the roof of their hut

[80]

threw three hand grenades inside and silenced the enemy.

He returned to his machine gun, slung it over his back and tried to catch up with his comrades. He lost his way, and only just before daybreak, as the North Star appeared from under the clouds in the pale morning sky, did he manage to join his comrades.

All night long, climbing over rocks the frontier guards moved back toward their pre-arranged assembly point. They kept their pursuers under fire and on their way cut the enemy's telephone lines. By morning all of them had gathered in a ravine under a high crag. Tronin was the last to arrive. Two of our men had perished in the battle near the mud huts. Two others were wounded; they had dressed their own wounds and with clenched teeth walked unaided to the assembly point. All the others were alive and in good health although tired, frozen and ready to fall asleep on the spot.

Behind them were the blown up bridge, three demolished houses, nineteen smashed mud huts, ten destroyed cars and two hundred enemy corpses scattered on the white snow. Commissar Prokhorov and Commander Likhushin counted their men. Half an hour later, no one remained near the rock. New snow covered our tracks. The frontier guards disappeared as suddenly as they had come, taking a path that they alone knew. It is their business to know such paths— that is what we have frontier guards for!

[81]

Namesakes

****

NOWHERE ON THE FRONT are the days as short and the nights as long as they are here. Our front extends thousands of miles southwards; but north of us there is nothing but the icy sea rolling its cold surges up to Spitzbergen. The land front breaks off here on the rocky shores of Musta-Tunturi.

As this was written, the battles for the Musta-Tunturi mountain chain entered upon their sixth month. They began in the summer, when the cold cliffs covered with a sparse growth of lichens were still occasionally warmed by the rare northern sun; they continued in the fall when wild northern gales tripped our daredevils as they climbed on ropes from ledge to ledge, and hurled them against the rocks; and they continued now, in winter, when snowdrifts covered the precipices and the stones cracked from the cold and the water froze on the edge of your cup before you had time to raise it to your lips.

The seasons came and went, but our companies still fought amid the rocks of Musta-Tunturi without yielding an inch of its stony, subpolar ground to the enemy. And the operational surveys still mention the "seventh frontier post," "a nameless lake" and "the upper plateau."

The ground here was measured inch by inch. We could recognize every stone, every crack, by its shape or its feel. We could not afford to make the slightest mistake here. For instance, to crawl thirty yards beyond our post at night would have been fatal. Here thirty yards was the distance that separated us from the enemy. At some points this distance stretched to fifty yards, only rarely to a hundred yards. The enemy came very close, as close as he could, right up to the ridge of the mountains. He thought that he would gain another one hundred, fifty or thirty yards, pass over the ridge and break through to the plain. But it was those very thirty yards that he had failed to win during all those months of fighting.

The Germans were so close that we could hear them talking.

Here it was impossible to dig into the ground, because there was no ground, only stones. And so the trenches were constructed upwards. In crevices between the rocks arose obstacles made of piled-up

[83]

stones, and later entire walls, a yard thick, with embrasures. The narrow ridge of the mountains, bare as a table, became No Man's Land. Every inch of it was under fire from two sides—our fire from the northern slopes, the enemy's fire from the southern slopes. And even before the long mountain lake situated on the plateau was frozen, tin cans of water had to be pulled up by ropes from below. The fifteen yards from our positions to the lake were impassable.

We paid with tens of lives for every yard of these rocks that we conquered. To recapture a lost yard also cost a bloody price. If one soldier had one second of cowardice or indecision, it might cost the lives of dozens of his comrades the following day. A trench occupied by the Germans today had to be retaken tomorrow. There was no place to withdraw to here. Here one must win or die. Die, but hold out.

In five months of battles a stern race of warriors was reared on the rocks of Musta-Tunturi, warriors who knew not how to retreat but knew how to look death in the eyes every day, every hour, every minute. Here calm, fearless men were trained, masters of hand-grenade throwing and hand-to-hand combat; men accustomed to live for weeks without fire, in frozen stony crevices; men who know how to wait for days for an opportunity to inflict "silent death," with a noiseless blow of the dagger—how to finish off an enemy who had fallen asleep even for one minute.

Where brave exploits, privations and danger are an everyday affair, people do not talk much about them.

They cease noticing them in themselves or others. And if they ever utter a few short words of praise, you may be sure that behind them there is a long series of daring deeds.

Just as everywhere else on the front, in every sector of it, so here, on Musta-Tunturi, there was one name that was mentioned first, with which every story of an unusual exploit began and ended. This name was Danilov, or more accurately, the Danilovs—for there were two of them: Sergeant Alexander Danilov, an immense, silent, placid boy from Leningrad, and Sergeant Ivan Danilov, an indefatigable, thick-set fellow from near Penza.

Accident had brought these two namesakes together almost at the end of the world, in the rocks of Musta-Tunturi, and their valor had made their name a by-word. Although they fought on different peaks, and knew each other only by hearsay, they were somehow tied by their common name. Each of them separately won fame for it and both of them defended its honor.

In a dugout, the commissar of the artillery regiment told me of his former sound-detector expert, Alexander Danilov, now a scout.

"It's a pity you won't see him," he said, "he's in the hospital. Five wounds. I don't expect him back for another two weeks . . ."

He did not finish his sentence. The low door banged, then the boards lining the narrow corridor creaked, and an enormous man in a sheepskin coat with a helmet on his head entered the dugout. He was so enormous

[85]

that the big sheepskin coat looked almost like a baby's shirt on him. His heavy hands seemed to be bursting out of his sleeves, and his jacket spanned across his chest at every button.

"Sergeant Danilov returning from the hospital," he reported in a deep voice.

"Sit down, sit down, speak of the devil and the devil is here. . . ." The commissar with evident pleasure looked at Danilov's broad stolid pink face. "You've come back rather quickly. . . ."

"Not at all, I should say rather slowly, Comrade Commissar," said Danilov calmly. "The doctors think that if you have five wounds you should stay with them forever. They can't get it into their heads that for a man of my build five wounds is just like one wound for a man of average build."

"You should have explained that to them," said the commissar, smiling.

"I did. That's why they discharged me," said Danilov with conviction.

I asked him to tell me about the last battle in which he had taken part.

Just as unhurriedly and painstakingly as he did everything else, Danilov sat down on the earthen step, rolled himself a cigarette and began to speak in the even voice of a man who remembers everything and is surprised at nothing.

"I was given thirty men (there's no room for more than that number to deploy) and ordered to dislodge the Finns. We set out on the night of the 12th. Part of the way we crawled along crevices, part of the way in the open. There's nothing you can do about it, a stone is a stone and you can't bury yourself in it. That's that. I ran over first, the boys followed me. The fire was heavy. A few of the boys remained behind, they didn't run across. I went back for them so that they would feel happier running across the plateau with their commander. One of them, Borislavski, was wounded immediately. He cried: 'Comrade, Comrade Commander!' I said: 'Shut up, shut up!' There was no reason to make so much noise, was there? I bandaged his wound, and that was that.

"In one hour we lost thirteen men out of thirty in killed and wounded. I threw many hand grenades, then I ran out of them. I was wounded by bomb fragments in the side, the hand and the shoulder blade. The boys bound up the wounds and there I was with sixteen men.

"I sent six of them to the left, to prevent the enemy from outflanking us, and held the position with ten men.

"The second day at 5:00 P.M., the Finns opened an attack. During the day I had collected a lot of hand grenades—about sixty of them—and piled them up close to me. I had also collected three rifles. I wasn't badly supplied as you see. Then two more of my men got killed, my sergeant and Private Tereitsev.

"Meanwhile the Finns came closer and closer. I arranged all my hand grenades within reach, in a circle, so that they would not all blow up at once in case of an

accident. I can throw them farther than most people. . . ."

"How far can you throw them?"

"Fifty yards, a little more. In peacetime I threw them
fifty-six yards. I thought I wouldn't do worse here, and
perhaps even better, in the heat of battle.

"The Finns began to shower us with hand grenades,
and fire at us with machine guns and mortars. At the
edge of the little plateau there was a rock. I sat behind it. Behind me was a slope, in front of me a stony
plateau, and at the other end of that plateau were the
Finns.

"I stood between two rocks. They were big rocks,
they came up to other people's heads, but they reached
only to my chest. The boys took cover below me, there
was no reason to risk everyone's life in vain. As for me
I could hold out for the time being.

"The plateau was about thirty yards wide, I couldn't
afford to let the Finns take it. I began to use my hand
grenades. Then the boys began to load them for me
and hand them to me from below. I never saw a Finn
stand up to his full height. As soon as I saw one get
halfway up, I hurled a hand grenade, and he was seen
no longer. That was in the beginning, later there was
so much smoke from hand grenades and mines, that
almost nothing could be seen.

"You couldn't see anything, but you could hear the
click of the capsule—that meant a bomb was going to
be thrown. Then the long wooden handle would flash

in the smoke, and I would throw my own grenade in the direction from which the other missile had come.

"Almost all our hand grenades were spent. Then I lay behind the rock on top of the boys. You see how big I am, I covered almost all of them with my body. Maybe I'm a trifle heavy for them, I thought, but then nothing would hit them through me.

"Then I was again wounded in the fingers of my right hand, in the neck and in one eye. The eye was drenched with blood, I couldn't see anything. I got up and hurled our last three hand grenades haphazardly, and just then I heard Russian voices behind me—reinforcements had arrived. I said: 'At last!' I couldn't say anything else. . . .

"When the shooting subsided a little, I crawled down to the Commander. 'Well,' I told him, 'what shall I do? I haven't got any bandage. I used all mine up on Borislavski.'

"He ordered me to crawl to the ambulance. There the boys helped me, bandaged me and gave me water to drink—I hadn't had a swallow of water for two days. That's the whole exploit. . . ."

"Yes, that's all there was to it," confirmed the commissar, "except for one little detail. Danilov forgot to tell you that after his first wound he couldn't move his right hand. And so for two days he fought with one hand, his left hand. That's why the boys loaded his hand grenades for him. He couldn't do it himself."

"That's not quite so," Danilov observed. "I couldn't move my hand, but I still could move my fingers. I held my hand tightly between my knees, so it wouldn't shake, and then I could move my fingers."

At Danilov's side lay the Finnish helmet he had just removed from his head.

"I'm wearing this one," he said, pushing it contemptuously with his foot. "My own was pierced by a grenade, so I took this one. For the moment it serves me better than it did its previous owners. . . ."

A few days later I met the other Danilov.

This was in the foothills of Musta-Tunturi. The low northern sun had barely appeared when it began to set behind the ridge.

Sergeant Ivan Danilov, a sturdy little man in a great coat sprinkled with snow, stood against a background of rocks and crevices. He had just returned from our advanced positions. He spoke vigorously, nodding his head in the direction of Musta-Tunturi, and he made quick, descriptive gestures as though trying to accelerate his tale.

"There was one machine gun that was a real plague to our company, you just couldn't get by it. Then two of us, Private Volkov and myself, went up to destroy that gun which was keeping us from going forward. We crawled along crevices up to the gun and blew up three Germans with our hand grenades. Another one ran away, but we overtook him with a bullet. There we were on the hilltop. We had two automatic rifles. We took cover and waited for an attack. Building trenches with stones we made ourselves a perfect dugout, a real bastion. It's easy up here, what with all the stones lying around.

"At first they fired at us with rifles and machine guns. When they saw that this had no effect, they began to fire at us with a whole battery of mortars. They smashed up the entire hilltop, we were the only things on it they didn't hit; their aim wasn't bad at all.

"At nightfall, Volkov went down to establish liaison, and I stayed up there. In front of me there was a little hollow, and beyond another hilltop, occupied by the Germans. Between me and them there was only that little hollow, nothing else. I sat on my rock for a whole day. I didn't want to leave it, I stayed there on purpose, thinking to myself: now we're going to see what kind of rock you are, Musta-Tunturi. And so I sat there until our boys came up from all sides. And just as I began to run out of cartridges, and was thinking I'd have to fight it out with my fists."

"Why don't you tell how you were wounded?" someone asked.

"But that was before. . . ."

"And your head wound was before, too?"

"No, my wound in the head was after. Anyway it doesn't matter. A bomb burst right against my helmet, I was just bespattered. It's true there was a lot of blood, but the wound was superficial, nothing at all. This is how it happened. I was sitting there holding out against the attack until it grew dark. Then our boys came up, and a hand grenade fight started. We began to climb at the given signal—two shots with a pistol. The Germans pelted us with hand grenades from above. It's more fun to walk under that kind of fire. Your movements are livelier. We got up to the German trenches, showered them with hand grenades, and then I picked up a rifle and six hand grenades, and hid in a crevice.

"Five minutes later they passed to the counter-attack. One German rushed straight at me. I only wanted to wound him and drag him up to where I was, as a prisoner. But I fumbled with my rifle, and he hid behind a rock. I had to blow him up with a hand grenade, otherwise he might have run away for all I know. Then three more of them rushed at me, so I cut them down with my automatic. I've a good automatic, it rattles regularly, like a sewing machine. Then the rest of the Germans noticed me, I was on the extreme left. They began to crawl up to me, throwing hand grenades. They corrected their aim; threw them straight at my head. Their bombs sizzle for a long time, all I had to do was to take them by the handles and throw them back. I threw three such bombs, and the fourth hit the edge of a rock and fell on my helmet. I shook it down on the stones and it blew up right in front of my face. I was wounded in the face, cheeks, neck, leg. I was drenched in blood. I threw my last hand grenade and went back, shooting as I went.

"I crawled to the ledge, and there I saw two boys, wounded, one in a leg, the other in the back. One cried out: "Bandage me if you can, I'm bleeding white." I used my bandage up on him. I was about to tear up my shirt for myself, but first I asked him whether I was still bleeding freely. 'No,' he said, 'it's stopping.' Well, if that's the case, I thought, I won't bandage myself, so I didn't tear up my shirt.

"One of them had left his rifle in the hollow. I had to crawl back after it, for what kind of soldier would he be without a rifle? As soon as I came back, a fragment of a mortar shell hit me in the small of the back. And then the Germans began to shell the whole place.

"What was to be done? We had to go one way or another. One of the wounded men was able to walk, and I took the other on my back. The Germans sent over another mortar shell. I threw myself on all fours and lay down on my belly, like a snake, and that was that. The wounded man on my back was shaken a bit. 'Never mind,' I said to him, 'hold on Vanka! (we called him Vanka).' And so I brought them back to our lines, I remember that much very well. What happened afterward I don't remember so well. I lay down and couldn't breathe, I was so tired. That was the kind of battle we had."

The sun was setting over Musta-Tunturi. Slinging his automatic across his shoulders, Ivan Danilov looked southward. His face expressed disappointment. This tireless man could not remain still on one spot. He would gladly have returned to Musta-Tunturi then and there and spent the night with his rifle in his hand, in an ambush, together with his namesake and unknown friend, Alexander Danilov, who had just returned from the hospital.

It was growing dark now. Among the cliffs of Musta-Tunturi, lighting their indentations for a moment, flashed brief bursts of trench mortar shells.

A Holiday Night

****

On the night of November 6 a small detachment of scouts was leaving for an expedition far behind the enemy lines. The chief of our reconnaissance gathered the members of the expedition together in a crowded room at headquarters.

"According to our latest reports the Germans are engaged in regrouping their forces here, on the coast. You will land at night and check whether their battery and covering troops are still on the northern cape. If they are no longer there, destroy everything they have built, and if they are there, destroy them as well as their installations."

He looked around at the faces of his men. "This night, from November sixth to seventh you'll have to spend behind the enemy lines. Try to make it festive for yourselves and disastrous for the enemy."

The scouts drew up in the yard, almost entirely invisible in their white cloaks against the snow. With the chief's permission, I accompanied the detachment that night as a rank-and-file soldier.

The little cutter was tossed about violently. Although full of water it advanced at full speed to give us more time for the raid and to reach the landing spot at the precise moment when the darkness would become complete.

Luden, the commander of the detachment, a former cavalryman and a man of gay disposition, looked with hostility at the full moon which was rising above the horizon.

"There is dialectics for you," he said, pointing at the broad path of moonlight which spread over the waves; "what gladdened you in your youth saddens you in your mature age. The moon . . . For five months now she has been my personal enemy, and yet in olden times. . . . Ah, what's the use of remembering!"

The cutter was now sailing along the enemy shore. A week earlier I myself had seen the Germans firing shrapnel at one of our motorboats for two hours. But that night everything was quiet. Only to the side, farther west, one could see short flashes of the guns of a destroyer that was bombarding the coast.

The tide began to ebb. The cutter reached a stony shoal under the water and could not come closer to shore. A tiny boat was lowered and a gangway thrown to it from the cutter. A second trap was lowered from "Tuzik" directly into the water—it couldn't reach the shore anyway. Then two Red sailors from the crew of the cutter without waiting for orders jumped into the icy water, which was waist-deep, in order to help the scouts disembark.

The scouts had a difficult task before them. It was necessary for them to be dry, so the sailors carefully carried their comrades to the shore, one after another, as if they were children. This was a friendly gesture, done without comment and without any expectation of gratitude, a routine demonstration of the solidarity among the men of our different services.

There was a heavy surf, and many of us, including myself, had no luck, our boots got full of water, but we were at least spared the necessity of bathing up to the waist in the freezing surf. We gathered in silence on the shore and advanced in a long file. To reach our objective we had to walk six or seven miles over steep rocks covered with snow and ice. The wet flaps of our cloaks instantly turned into ice and rustled and crackled as we climbed. In an effort to reduce them to silence, which was essential for us, we rubbed them with our fingers as we walked.

At the head of the line walked three men who had been here more than once. They looked into every crevice and examined every stain on the snow, searching for footprints. But there were none, except the tiny imprints of a hare and little stripes similar to human footprints on the steep slope along which the otters rolled down to the water.

The rocks were piled up one on another. From a distance it seemed that you couldn't get past them, but when you came closer you always discovered a crevice or a ledge with the help of which you could climb another ten yards upwards. Worst of all were the bare, almost vertical, slopes covered with a smooth layer of snow. Swept constantly by winds, this snow is as hard as stone and as slippery as ice. One clumsy move, and you rolled down a good ten yards.

Luden, who was walking in front of me, slipped and immediately rolled down. Scout Khrabrin, trying to help him, also slipped and rolled five yards lower. When they at last managed to get up someone said in a whisper: "A real Suvorov pass." The commander who was limping after his fall but whose spirits were as high as ever turned around: "I forbid you to use that word," he said. "Why?" "Because first one must achieve results like Suvorov's, and only then speak of Suvorov passes."

At last we were given a short rest. We lay on the snow in the shadow of an enormous rock. Someone looked at his watch—it was exactly midnight. November 7. . . . Yes, the seventh, the anniversary of the revolution. Someone began to reminisce in a whisper of how he had spent this night one year before in his home in the Dniepropetrovsk district.

Far ahead in the white fog we could discern the opposite shore. For an instant the headlights of a car flashed from over there, a blue spark was quickly extinguished.

"It's our men driving," someone said.

And at that moment it was somehow important for all of us to know that somewhere over there, on our shores, our men were driving our cars.

Our ice-covered cloaks now proved extremely useful: they stood away from us stiffly, protecting us from the penetrating wind.

We had barely resumed our march when Kovalev, who was first in line, ran into a communication wire which connected the Germans' advance positions with headquarters. We put a stone under the cable, cut it with a dagger and buried the ends in the snow. Let them find it now. As we walked the next kilometre we repeated this operation three or four times.

We were quite close now; a group of tall, stony mounds descended to the narrow cape which protruded far into the water. We divided into three groups and crawled ahead, going around the mounds from three sides and gradually moving upwards. The night was clear; in addition to the moon, opalescent northern lights illumined the sky from end to end. And yet at thirty paces the men crawling on the snow looked merely like rocky ledges covered with frost. Even the dark stains of our boots and automatics did not betray us. On this stony ground, they looked like stones protruding from under the snow.

We went higher and higher up the slope. If the Germans had been there, they would have noticed us by now, in this clear night. But everything was silent. At last we reached the first mud huts. Everything seemed to indicate that they had been abandoned a day or two before. Hanging from the roofs there were lamps and lanterns, and in the brick stoves were half-burnt pieces of wood. Nearer to the cape, on a cliff, stood a few buildings that looked like warehouses. All the doors to these were hermetically closed.

Someone asked impatiently if he could "blow them up with a little hand grenade." But Luden, avoiding premature noise, said, No. Inzartsev, his assistant, took a few men and they smashed the doors with the butts of their rifles. The buildings were indeed warehouses: they contained stores of food, flour, bricks of tea wrapped in transparent paper with German water-marks, sacks of coffee, chickory, egg powder and straw-covered bottles of spirits. The stores were half full.

Not far from these stores, we found a crippled mountain gun. An abandoned gun could be explained, but abandoned German stores with provisions—that was surprising. No, we concluded, the Germans have not yet gone away for good. Apparently they were only regrouping their units, and in a day or two a new company was doubtless due to arrive at this deserted section of the front. It was for this company that these provisions, brought here with great difficulty over the single mule track, had been left.

Of course, it could not be otherwise. I involuntarily recalled the German captain whom we had captured a few days before. He had sat there, dirty, ragged, in a worn out field-grey uniform and unwashed shirt. He had been fed for a day on our adequate rations, yet seizing the moment when his questioner bent over the record he surreptitiously drew out of his pocket a lump of sugar that had been given him and greedily bit into it. Catching my glance he began to chew faster, obviously ashamed—as an officer of the German army he felt uncomfortable at being caught in this act—yet he continued to bite into the piece of sugar. His craving for it was stronger than any other feeling.

I involuntarily recalled this scene when I saw the stores with German provisions. Of course, they would return here. If they had decided to clear out entirely they would have scraped everything together, down to the last handful of flour and the last grain of coffee.

Luden ordered the radio operator to get in touch with our cutter which was cruising somewhere off shore. In the silence we heard the barely perceptible dots and dashes hammered out by our apparatus. We decided to burn the stores. When the cutter we had summoned came close to the shore everything was ready to be set on fire. With three other men I remained ashore while the rest of the group embarked. Then we poured gasoline over the boxes and planks we had piled up like a pyramid in the center of the stores, and set it on fire. As we went down to the shore, jumping from stone to stone, we saw the reddish flames penetrating through the narrow cracks of the doors.

It was still dark but daybreak was at hand. The

cutter noiselessly moved away from the shore. We were some distance out in the stormy bay when the stores at last began to blaze for fair. The fire spread to unexpectedly impressive dimensions. Over the rocks soared an immense pillar of fire, now rising, now falling. Inside something was exploding with tremendous force. Apparently, in addition to provisions, military supplies were stored up somewhere in the cellars. Well, so much the better. They would remember this festive night all the longer.

We were nearing our own shores.

It was daybreak when we disembarked from the cutter and marched through the town, numb with cold, but gay in spirit. We had met the holiday well. It was worth remembering. The holiday night was over now. Above the doorways of the houses fluttered our own red flags, with their hammers and sickles familiar since the days of our childhood.

The Last Night

★★

IT SEEMED THAT EVERYTHING in the town was just as usual that night. As usual, the "Latest News," a daily published under the auspices of the German command, had come out. As usual, it contained the cheerful announcement that the German troops had captured seventeen million square kilometres of Russian territory, that is to say, all of European Russia and one-third of Siberia, as far as Yakutsk. On the fourth page, "Mechanics, Inc." advertised its readiness to accept new shareholders. As usual, Major A. S. Gurzinov, having turned in his daily report to the German commandant, was sleeping peacefully in his new apartment, furnished by the obliging Germans.

Doctor Rudel was at work at his desk under the

light of a green-shaded lamp. He was summing up the results of a medical examination of fifty young girls from Feodosya destined to work in the house of prostitution that was to be inaugurated the next day. In celebration of this solemn occasion, Messrs. the German officers had assembled in some private apartments and were drinking French brandy around the Christmas trees.

The cold December wind rattled the most recent placard posted on the walls and fences by the German command: "It has come to our knowledge that a number of houses in the town of Feodosya have been mined and are to be blown up. The population is hereby requested to give the addresses of all mined houses to the military authorities of Feodosya. Those who contribute toward preventing the prepared explosions by reporting the facts accurately and promptly will be suitably rewarded. In the future, for every blown-up house, according to the damage done, no less than thirty hostages will be shot. Signed, The German Commandant."

In the anti-tank ditch behind the Bedrizov cement factory, lashed by the wind and lightly covered with recently fallen snow, lay nine hundred and seventeen bodies of Russians, Tartars and Jews, aged twelve to eighty, who had been machine-gunned here on December 8. At the other end of the town, this time not in a ditch but on the ground, lay two hundred and thirty Crimeans, shot nine days later.

Mr. Shaposhnikov, the Russian chief of police, only

recently, in a report to the German army authorities, had proved scientifically that the more Crimeans the Germans executed the less trouble they would have. Now he was working complacently at his desk writing a new detailed report showing that the sect of the Karaimes deserved a similar fate. Under the windows of the mayor's apartment, on a transom between a telegraph pole and a tree, swung the bodies of two men, who belonged to the last batch of the hanged.

In brief, in sunny Crimea, in the town of Feodosya, everything was "in good order" that night.

The first shot rang out at exactly three minutes past midnight. The Red Marines approached the port of Feodosya noiselessly and from many directions. The first man to land on the snow-covered pier was Red Marine Evtushenko. The rat-tat-tat of his automatic which swept over the German sentries walking back and forth along the pier was the first noise that awakened the town.

The raid was daring and unexpected. The cutters came close to shore. Climbing up the slippery, ice-covered slabs, one marine after another jumped on the Feodosya jetty. The landing was met with fire; our men suffered losses, but having reached the long-yearned-for Crimean shores, they fought like lions. They clung to the jetty with only one thought: Feodosya must be taken!

Before them stood a stone wall protecting the ports. The vanguard detachment was to make its way to this wall, capture it and hold it at any cost, at the cost of their lives if need be, until the infantry landed. With a handful of marines, Evtushenko ran to the wall, zig-zagging among the ruins of blown-up stores. In one crooked lane they bumped into seven Germans.

"Surrender!" cried the Germans.

"Here we are!" cried Evtushenko with a kind of wild gaiety, and although the Germans were quite close to him, he flung his last precious "lemon" at their feet.

Sergeant Kuzenko and his boys ran to the other harbor wall, disregarding all obstacles. There were no stores on the stretch they had to race through, it was an open field strewn with stones and covered with ice over which German bullets were sputtering angrily. With Spondayko and Kriukov, he ran up to the wall. He pulled himself up and from the top saw that a group of Germans were running on the other side. The wall was too high. The Ukrainians, who were quick-witted fellows, rolled an empty iron barrel over to the wall. Kuzenko jumped upon it and hurled his first hand grenade, which he followed by twelve others. His two comrades below charged the hand grenades and passed them up to him, and he hurled them with gusto at the feet of the German riflemen, where they burst with a thunderous noise. These thirteen hand grenades were a real "devil's dozen" for the Germans. The following morning, fifty frozen and twisted corpses of Nazis were found near the wall at this spot, while on the other side stood the iron barrel riddled with bullets.

Forward, forward, always forward, marched Sergeant Patusin, of the first squad. His automatic fired furiously at the Germans, paying them back for everything: for his native Odessa, which he will reconquer, for the blood he had shed there, for his old wound which still ached. Marine Kambiev, gravely wounded in one leg, was limping, but still shooting from his automatic as he stumbled heavily, staining the snow with his blood.

"I'll get to that wall lame or not lame," he muttered through his teeth, breathing heavily, firing at the Germans and shouting ancient Russian words which are never printed in books, but which, it is generally agreed, are most helpful when you go into an attack.

These marines had volunteered for this assignment; they were the first to return to the Crimea. They were led by two brave men: Commander Aidinov, an Azerbaijanian, and Commissar Ponamarev, a Russian. The enemy fire was fierce, and, say what you will, to take a town from the sea is no easy matter. It was hard to conquer the short stretch between the mooring and the wall. Sergeant Ivannikov, and Kochetkov, Shavrin and Permiak, died the death of the brave before reaching it. A few other sailors whom the wind carried to the settlement of Sarigol also lost their lives. These Russian boys disembarked fearlessly on snow-covered stones near the shore. They were surrounded and fought to the last cartridge. They died silently, clenching their teeth, as is fitting for men who are reconquering their native soil inch by inch at the price of their lives.

But nothing could stop the marines. They got pos-

session of the wall, jumped over it and rushed forward
into the town, along the black streets where the cannon
thundered. They took house after house, apartment
after apartment. They made their way up narrow stair-
cases, fought on landings, in hallways, in rooms. Every
one of them fought like ten men, for all they knew was:
"We must take Feodosya!"

That night it was hard to take a live German. Three
times, Captain Blinov gave orders that an enemy officer be brought to him, and three times his men came
back empty-handed.

"I can't," said a tall sailor, without a helmet, his head
bandaged with a bloodstained handkerchief, as he
stood before the captain. "I can't see one and not
kill him. So many of my comrades have perished
by their hands, and I must let him live? Do as you wish,
comrade commander, but I have not the strength to
let a German live."

For the fourth time the commander sent two ser-
geants, Tkach and Gerbov, to get a prisoner. They
broke into a house on Italian Street, in front of which,
without taking cover from the flying bullets, stood an
old woman with smooth hair begging the Russians to
come in, to come in and kill—these were the exact
words she used—kill three officers who were hiding in
this house.

Tkach and Gerbov broke into the apartment. They
were met with shots. Two German officers who had decided to die with arms in their hands got their wish.
Stepping across their bodies, Tkach and Gerbov en-

tered the next room. The third German dressed only in his underwear was lying under the bed; on the back of his chair hung his tunic with captain's stripes and an Iron Cross. The wind blew the snow in through the smashed window. The marines pulled the German from under the bed. He was comical, this scrawny fellow in silk underdrawers, who shivered with cold and was soon covered with snow from the open window. He was taken just as he was to headquarters, the first prisoner to be captured in Feodosya.

The marines continued to move forward along the streets, and behind them now thundered the guns of the warships which had come up close to the jetty and from which Major Andreev's infantry had disembarked. Having made their way through streets which were blocked with overturned cars, through courtyards swept by automatic riflemen from all sides, the infantrymen rushed on still farther, beyond the town, into the mountains, on the heels of the retreating Germans.

Daybreak came. Commissar Ponomarev walked down one of the streets along the shore to his headquarters in the *Kommandantur* which had just been recaptured. Now he was master of the town and he had to organize its government. As he walked, he glanced at the German staff cars parked at the entrance to the *Kommandantur*. He paid no attention to the stray bullets which grazed him. He had become accustomed to their whistling. People were emerging from their cellars. On Lenin Street, the commissar, a huge, broad-shouldered man whose arms were encumbered with rifles and hand grenades, was accosted by a thin, ten-year-old girl.

"Little uncle," she said, "may I wear my necktie again now? I've got it here already."

Unclenching her tiny, frozen, blue fingers she showed the commissar a miniature Pioneer badge in the palm of her hand—which could be used as a tie-clip.

"You may," said the commissar. "Everything is all right now."

He wanted to add something—an affectionate, kindly word, but he suddenly remembered that he was the commissar of the town, that there was still shooting in the streets and that he must re-establish power here. He waved his hand and, stepping heavily over the bodies of German soldiers, walked towards his office.

A Common Language

✦✦

WE FIRST CAUGHT SIGHT of them in the air. The Germans had attempted to make their third big raid on the city since the outbreak of war. Not a single Junker got through though. They were sent hurtling, crashing down onto the cliffs, far beyond the reaches of the city.

Now they were on their way back from the hard-fought battle. Overhead we could see our Soviet fighter planes, and alongside them were strange machines with tricolor circles on the fuselage—British fighter planes.

The next morning we paid a visit to the aerodrome. The British planes were lined up alongside ours.

The aerodrome was hemmed in on all sides by hills—

[111]

the landing field had been literally hewn out of the rocks. The hangars, snuggling under the cliffs, were covered over with grass, boulders and earth. The airmen stood beside their Hurricanes, in full kit, ready to take off at a moment's notice.

The first flakes of snow were falling. Some of the Britishers were kicking a football about in the middle of the field.

The tokens on the collars of their tunics indicated that many of the pilots were volunteers. The badges on the sleeves of others showed that they came from Australia or Canada. They had, in fact, come from all parts of the globe. The commander himself, a thick-set, sturdily built man with greying hair and a tanned face —Lieutenant-Colonel Neville Isherwood—hailed from New Zealand.

The war had brought him here, to the far north, thousands of miles away from his native land. But he, an old soldier, was not at all dissatisfied.

For years he had been a test pilot. There was not a single make of plane now in use in the British forces the world over that he had not tested in the air. The red ribbon of the highest award in the British air force embellished his modest grey tunic. He had seen service in the Sudan, in Burma, in Egypt, in France, in Abyssinia. And now he was here—brought here by a soldier's *esprit de corps* and a soldier's hatred for the common foe.

He told us with a tinge of pride that his "wing" included fliers from all the countries of the British

Commonwealth: Australians, Canadians, Rhodesians, South Africans, men from the West Indies, Scotsmen, Welshmen, Irishmen.

And now they were fighting here, fighting stubbornly against the dastardly "Jerries" as they had nicknamed the Germans.

"We are fighting here just as stubbornly as we fought in England," Lieutenant-Colonel Isherwood said to me, "fighting together with your men and under the command of your general. If you intend to write this up please mention that it's an honor to be fighting here under the command of such a brave and experienced soldier. Even back in England I marveled at the staunch fight the Russian people were putting up and now I am glad to be doing my bit here with them. On land we speak in different languages, but directly we go up your fliers and ours immediately find a common language—and that's what's most important."

And that indeed is what is most important. On land the Britishers are rather a taciturn lot. When I asked the major, the commander of a squadron, who had a dozen or so "Jerries" to his record, how he had done it, he said to me after a moment's thought and without even a trace of a smile, literally the following:

"Sheer luck. When we went up, well, just at that very moment and in that particular locality, the 'Jerries' also showed up. They simply paid for this coincidence. That's all."

"That's all." This phrase has become international

among our men and the British pilots. Neither like to go into details. "We went up, brought them down, got back—and that's all."

And if you want to learn the details of various feats of our airmen the best thing to do is to go to the Britishers, who, discarding their usual taciturnity, go into lengthy descriptions of the splendid fight put up by their Russian friends and neighbors.

If you want to know what the Britishers are doing, the best thing is to ask our men.

They will tell you how Captain Rooks, at the height of a battle, dived into a group of Messerschmidts and tackled nine enemy planes single-handed, how he fought, climbed, dived from an altitude of 3,000 metres down to the very sea level, bringing down one Messerschmidt and damaging another. They will tell you how Major Miller, who went up with his unit of six planes on a training spin, sighted fourteen Junkers heading for the aerodrome, how he immediately attacked the enemy, brought down three and scattered the rest.

They will tell you how, during a sudden raid on their aerodrome, Pilots Bush and Houghmans, with bombs bursting all around them, reached their planes and, speeding down the runway in between the yawning craters, went up and attacked the enemy.

The pilots of our fighter planes who are fighting shoulder to shoulder with the Britishers, here, in the far north, above the icy waters of the Barents Sea, above the bleak rocks of the Polar Circle, will tell you all this and more.

[114]

The pilots of our bomber planes speak with soldierly esteem and pride of the pilots of the British fighter planes who escort them on their raids far behind the enemy lines. No matter what the circumstances, they stick to them like true Britons; our pilots tell how, having brought them to their goal, they wait for them notwithstanding the terrific barrage put up by enemy anti-aircraft guns, hang on like leeches, warding off the attacks of the fascist fighter planes and, with the job finished, escort them back safely home.

However, their respect is mutual. The Britishers highly praise the Soviet bombers. To risk one's life is no easy matter. But they are ready to do so because they know that, here, the results are worth it. They know that no matter how stubborn the enemy's resistance may be, how heavy the odds, no matter in what weather, the Soviet bombers they escort will nevertheless get through and demolish their objective.

"I have only one complaint to make," Major Miller said to me with a smile.

"And what's that?"

"Against the crews of your anti-aircraft guns. They're such excellent marksmen that they often poach on our preserves. The last time, however, I became very friendly with them. It was misty, heavy clouds covered the sky, and we could not sight the 'Jerries.' Your gunners, however, fired with such precision, that, watching the shell-burst, we immediately spotted where the enemy was lurking."

In the underground canteen, the British pilots were

[115]

chatting and smoking, drinking tea, warming themselves up.

The fortunes of war had brought them here to the far north. Soldiers, in general, have a deep love for their own country and these, too, had brought with them to this remote spot a bit of old England. Inside the canteen we were given a selection of English songs and ditties. At the commander's observation point, on a crate which served as a desk for the field telephone, one of them had printed in bold letters some sort of inscription.

I asked one of the Englishmen to translate it for me.

Captain Cotton smiled.

"It's not so easy to translate," he said. "What's written on that box is the name of a famous London police station in which drunkards of all ranks and classes usually come to rest. The implication is that 'Jerries' of all ranks and classes—from Junkers to Messerschmidts—will find eternal rest on this bit of Russian soil."

The Britishers are a light-hearted lot and they fight light-heartedly. In their spare time they are not averse to a bit of fun. And in this inscription there is much of the traditional, good-natured and dry British humor.

There is the same sense of humor in the caricature pinned on the wall. It shows lanky Captain Rooks with his legs dangling out of a plane chasing after a group of "Jerries." Alongside is a sheet of foolscap: in

[116]

a neat hand is inscribed a record of enemy planes actually brought down, and also enemy planes which have been crippled and presumably destroyed. At the bottom of this truly authentic record is a drawing: it shows drops trickling into a bottle which is only one-third full.

"What is this supposed to mean?"

"The bottle? It's a bottle we split among the lot of us. We haven't brought down quite enough planes yet, that's why it's only one-third full. Our job is to fill it to the top and when that's done we'll crack a bottle of the real stuff." That was Lieutenant-Colonel Isherwood's reply to my question.

He opened his cigarette case and lit up.

"That's my wife," he said, passing me his cigarette case. In the inside lid was a miniature photograph. "I haven't seen her for ages and that's why I'm getting to be a heavy smoker, so as to see her more often. Everything would be fine here if only we had some mail. We haven't received a single letter from England yet. But that's a detail. The main thing just now is to fight. As for the letters they're sure to turn up some day. . . ."

We said goodbye to our hosts. On the way back we looked in at the headquarters of the Soviet Command.

What interested us was our general's opinion on the work of the Britishers.

"My opinion? Splendid men. They came here to fight and they're fighting like real soldiers. Staunch and disciplined men. There's one thing I have against

[117]

them—they don't like doing patrol duty. They say it's boring. They're always after me with requests to go up and escort our bombers on a raid on the enemy's lines. It's the same thing with our men. They also don't like patrolling the empty sky. They also keep on pestering me with requests to be up and away bombing the enemy. They're forever asking to be given the same jobs and when they come to grips with the enemy, well, both the Britishers and our men fight like lions. But look, they're off again."

And indeed, above our heads Soviet fighter planes and British Hurricanes were speeding on their way towards the enemy lines—Russian and British pilots who had found a common language up in the air.

The Rybachi and Sredni Peninsulas

★★★

IN THE FILES OF OUR POLITICAL DEPARTMENT, among the documents captured from the Germans, I found a ragged issue of a German newspaper. Its fourth page contained a story about the storming of the Sredni and Rybachi Peninsulas by brave mountain units. This story was particularly curious because right now we were sailing full speed on a little tugboat toward the shores of that same Rybachi Peninsula which, according to the German newspapers, had been captured by German mountain troops back in July. Yet the captain of the little tugboat, a scrawny and placid sailor in a faded sweater—the crew affectionately called him Petrusha—was not a bit afraid of being captured by the Germans. Unfortunately he had not read the *Voelkische Beobachter*, and so had no idea that the Germans had occupied the peninsula.

"I've been there several times, but I never saw a German on it," he said lazily chewing his cigarette. "It's true that they sometimes fired from the other shore, from Pikshuev Bay. That's true. But my canoe is no bigger than a flea—and how could you hit a flea with a cannon?"

Actually the tug was a rather difficult artillery target, particularly in weather such as we were experiencing, when amid the raging waves of Motovski Bay only the top of its big stack could be seen from a distance of fifty yards. I don't know the origin of the name "Motovski Bay," but everyone up here put forward the plausible explanation that it comes from the verb "motat," Russian for "toss," and among themselves the sailors call it familiarly "Motka,"—"Tossy."

All the ground around the landing places, the neighboring mounds and crevices, were peppered with craters from shells. Day after day, month after month, trying to interfere with the supply line of the defenders of the Rybachi and Sredni Peninsulas, the Germans had been bombing these shores. Thousands of tons of the metal they had thrown here littered the bottom of the bay.

"If we gathered all the iron they used to bomb this little port we could build another one entirely of metal," remarked a grey-headed lieutenant-colonel with the dry humor of an old man.

This was the extreme north, and all night long snow

[120]

had been falling. By morning the roads were so snow-bound that you couldn't even think of reaching Sredni from the Rybachi by car, until the snow-tractors had gone out.

"Just have a look at the map," said the commander of the port. "What a place for a native of Odessa! The Kola Peninsula is, so to speak, the nose of the continent, and the Rybachi is a wart on that nose. And so I am the commander of a wart. Yes, yes. And you'll have to stay with me for a whole day; the road won't be cleared till tomorrow. You'll have an opportunity to see how they bomb us."

Ginzburg looked at his watch and went toward the exit of the mudhut. "Usually it is just about now that they take a swill of their bean coffee and come over in their planes."

Five thousand yards above us, barely visible, a plane was actually circling overhead.

"In the beginning they flew lower, but our anti-aircraft shot down a few of them, so now they don't come below three thousand yards."

The plane traced a few more circles and without diving dropped half a dozen bombs. Pillars of water rose from the bay, and the plane turned westward.

"Now that we've been bombed," said the commander in a melancholy tone, while his eyes indifferently followed the disappearing plane, "we can have breakfast."

We didn't stay here overnight. The snow continued to fall, and we decided to go to the Sredni Peninsula by motorboat. The waves were so big that for whole minutes it seemed that the boat could not ride above them, but would have to go through them. Standing ankle deep in water and wrapped in a rubber coat, our helmsman, just to be on the safe side, steered close to shore. A man stood watch by the machine gun. Only a narrow sound separated us from the Germans. However, on a night such as this, we were unlikely to encounter any of them, the helmsman told me.

"A German won't venture out to sea in such weather. A Norwegian might go out, but he wouldn't take a German. The Norwegians don't like Germans."

"Don't like them?"

"That's what I said!"

After two hours, when the water in our boat was beginning to flood the motor we finally landed on the shores of the Sredni Peninsula. We had not a dry stitch on us. We had to climb up a steep path which soon was lost amid the rocks of a slippery, ice-covered slope. A sentry opened an invisible door to us.

Electric light, a captured Finnish stove made of wrought iron which breathed forth heat, the thick planks which formed the walls, ceiling and floor of the cabin, the broad tables with green-shaded lamps —everything pointed to the fact that our men were installed with all necessary comforts. Cozily sitting by the stove after a busy day, Colonel Vasilchikov drank glass after glass of strong tea "Moscow fashion."

"We haven't given them an inch," he said, marking

a line on the map of the peninsula with his finger nail. "To the left there's the bay; to the right the sea; in front of us, mountains. Everything that was in our hands, still is in our hands. And we have no intention of giving up anything. As for the Germans, well, they've been trying to dislodge us, of course. First their attempts were rash, now they've been more cautious. If you want details, have a look at our battle log. Everything is set down there."

Considering the matter settled, the colonel, who was not talkative, attacked his fifth glass of tea. The reason for his reluctance to talk proved the usual one with our officers: relating the battles for the peninsula, the colonel would willy-nilly have had to talk about himself.

In the first days of the war the Germans concentrated a few divisions and broke through on a twenty-mile front along the coastline in the direction of Murmansk. The narrow isthmus, the only path leading from the peninsula to the continent, was blocked by the Germans. The garrisons on the Rybachi and Sredni Peninsulas had been preparing for an attack from the sea. The appearance of the Germans from the land side took them by surprise. Only a few companies were defending the isthmus. The Germans hurled an entire division against them, trying to force the passage from the mountain to the isthmus by one blow and later spread out on the entire peninsula.

At that critical moment, the peninsula was saved by Colonel Vasilchikov's firm hand and iron will. He

gave orders to move the heavy shore batteries toward
the isthmus without losing a moment, and gathering
every available man, he himself hurried to the advance positions. He did not shrink from personally
shooting a coward on the spot, stopped the retreat of
our companies and hurled them against the Germans
in a counter-attack. Meanwhile the machine guns had
arrived, and, set up on the hills, they succeeded in
stopping the German advance. By evening our heavy
batteries had moved to their new positions. They
threw a wall of fire against the attacking German division, and one day later the situation was restored.
Not a single live German was left on the isthmus. On
the slopes of the hills, where one day earlier the German battalions had staged a "psychological attack,"
in close formation, there were piles of men mowed
down by machine-gun and artillery fire. From that
day on not a single German boot had succeeded in
trampling the stony ground of the Sredni and Rybachi Peninsulas. Month after month they tried to
break through, severe battles took place for the possession of the commanding heights on the continent
which adjoined the isthmus, but the Germans failed
to reach the isthmus itself.

We toured the two peninsulas for a few days. The
roads here are peculiar; they are not built, but bared—
the uneven spots are ironed out, boulders and clumps
of earth are removed until the bare rock appears. Often
the roads serve as drains; the water from the mountains breaking through the ice flows under the run-

ners of the sleighs. The telegraph poles are surrounded by pyramids of stones several feet tall to
protect them from being uprooted by the fierce winds.
The mud huts, shelters and command posts are all
built solidly, to last a long time, with supports of
heavy beams and iron plate.

The continuous arctic day interrupted only by
short, white dusks did not permit a moment of respite
or sleep during the entire summer. All the fortifications were erected in view of the enemy under his fire.
When these works were completed, the sappers began
to build roads and a hospital. In one month there
arose under the earth, or, more accurately, there grew
into the earth, an entire medical city. Wards with one
hundred and twenty beds, a reception room, an op-
erating room, laboratories. An underground hospital
of a peculiar type was created on the peninsula—it
was field and rear hospital simultaneously. Only those
patients who had to be hospitalized for more than six
weeks were sent off the peninsulas. Those who could
return to the ranks in six weeks or less were treated
right there.

Everything had gone underground: mud huts,
medical stations, garages, stables, stores. You could
travel mile after mile amid our troop dispositions and
see nothing but snow with reddish rocks protruding
from it.

Shore batteries camouflaged in the rocks of the
western coast of the peninsula sank German transports which followed the only existing route from

Kirkenes to Petsamo. Having discovered the approximate positions of our guns from their flashes, the Germans had tried a few times to get their transports through under cover of air bombardments. As soon as the transports sneaking along the shore approached Petsamo Bay, our batteries were bombed. But our artillerymen managed to fire upon the ships, jumping out of their shelters to their guns during the short intervals between two bombing raids. Having suffered the loss of a transport, the Germans began to bomb us without interruption, replacing each dive bomber as soon as it had exhausted its load. Then our artillerymen began to take shelter also in turn. One crew always remained outside during the bombardment and continued to fire at the transports.

Our heavy batteries that shelled the approaches to the isthmus caused great embarrassment to the Germans. Commander Skrobov remained in his observation post situated on the crest of the snowbound cliffs night and day. It took us more than two hours to get up there, mostly by crawling. The place was like an eagle's nest, and Skrobov's observers, hugging the cliff in their wide white cloaks, resembled big white birds. A constant furious harsh wind blows on this peak, every minute, hour, day, week and month of the year. It never stops. The observers' lips were cracked, their eyes were red and inflamed. But from their post, from this cliff open to the winds from four directions, all the roads and paths leading to the isthmus were perfectly visible.

Skrobov, a big, silent, rarely smiling man, had been nicknamed "the scientific worker" by his assistants, and actually carried on his work with scientific precision. Every ledge, every glade, every path, every square yard of territory, had its exact range taken. Wires connected this post with another observation post situated only five hundred yards from the German positions. And once when it was necessary, it was fifty yards behind the German lines. Artillery Lieutenant Loskutov accompanied by his radioman got behind the enemy and for three days corrected our fire from his hideout.

Skrobov had the obstinate mouth and the sharp eyes of a self-educated man. He had calculated and recorded everything. In this tiny mud hut carved out of the rock, this man, who not so long ago was a simple private and who had graduated from officers' school after only a correspondence course, managed to keep the complicated artillery records with absolute precision as though for qualifying examinations at officers' school.

The record of the losses he had inflicted on the Germans was impressive. In a short period of time our artillerymen had destroyed seven guns, seventeen trench mortars, twenty-three heavy machine guns, forty-six trucks, five command posts, two planes and 1,100 Germans. Incidentally, one of the planes our men destroyed was hit at eight miles, as it sat unsuspecting on the water near its own shore.

A November blizzard roared over the peninsula.

[127]

Snow and wind had taken possession of this territory until May. Snow covered up the entrances to our dug-outs, and every morning they had to be cleared. In another week, all our houses, including the chimneys, would be buried under a layer of snow. Night and day in the howling blizzard, the slopes of the mountain chain separating the continent from the isthmus were the scene of a bloody, stubborn battle between advance units. By night our men climbed up the rocks bringing hot food in thermoses to the advance posts. The wind never ceased, and in our mud hut, when we turned on the radio, we heard nothing but the howl and whistle of the wind.

All night long the winds blow from Norway. From Norway to Rybachi it is sixty miles. And from Soviet Russia to Norway, the distance is also: sixty miles.

My Land

★★★

HERE IT IS, the ground that seven months ago was called "No-man's land." A field covered with rusty, unmowed grass—eight hundred yards of ground which only yesterday lay between the barbed wire entanglements of the two armies. Now the barbed wire was torn in several places, the heavy tracks of caterpillars had deeply furrowed the earth—our tanks had moved forward here.

The first German lay with arms outspread in the ditch about a hundred yards in front of the first German trenches. He was doubtless one of a protective patrol; he must have been lying in his observation post concealed in the grass, when one morning the earth for many miles around shuddered from the first salvo of our heavy artillery. A hundred yards further were the smashed barbed wire entanglements, the trenches with their edges cut by caterpillar tracks, blockhouses with scattered fragments of wood. Our artillerymen must have been delighted to see the results of their work when they moved forward to take up their new positions.

Destructive barrage: black holes from shells that pierced the beams protecting the blockhouses; craters that made the earth level with the trenches; the ground was like a chessboard dotted with the regular black squares of explosions.

The village of Nikolskoye. Advance German fortifications. The trenches were littered with corpses of Germans half-buried in the earth: some were lying, some sitting, some standing—each had preserved the pose in which our barrage had surprised him. They had no opportunity to listen long to its deadly music. The village. This word usually evokes the image of huts and groups of trees and fences along the streets. What we saw here, however, was only a mass of ruins. Beyond this village we could see the horizon, nothing concealed it from our eyes. By the road, a gnarled stick with a tablet: "Nikolskoye." Beneath it lay the German inscription that had been torn down.

That was all—the rest was a heap of ruins, some dating from last year, overgrown with grass, some fresh—fragments of brick, glass, pieces of iron twisted by fire. Not even the chimneys usually left standing by the Germans were to be seen here, everything had been razed. Only the skeletons of burnt, mutilated German cars were strewn on both sides of the road; the Germans had tried to flee in various directions when our artillery overtook them.

To the left, close to the road, stood a German "Opel." A shell had torn out its motor, but its body was intact. Some wash had been carefully hung up on it to dry—a woman's jacket, a pair of coarse rags used in place of stockings. Beside the car, around a little fire, a man and a woman were frying cakes: the first inhabitants of Nikolskoye who had returned to their hearths. It was a bitter return. They had come here on foot with bundles containing their miserable belongings on their shoulders. They had come and found nothing except this German car on which they hung their clothes to dry. They had covered the broken windows with pieces of plywood and would use the car to shelter themselves from the rain and the wind. A thin blue smoke rose from a pile of bricks. In the pot water was boiling. Not a gay fireplace, but still a fireplace. Our native land, no matter how defiled, remains our native land, and people return to their hearths no matter what happens.

Beyond Nikolskoye, a temporary bridge spanned a deep ravine. Here everything had been dug up by airbombs. The Germans had been trying to hinder our movements on this road. With a quick staccato, similar to the popping of corks, automatic anti-aircraft were firing. Overhead, a Junker turned back and hid in the clouds. At the edge of the road were

[131]

little black mounds: anti-tank mines. Nearby, sappers and mine-removers were at work. This was not excessive caution: a tractor that had left the road had just been blown up by a mine.

Beyond the ravine, a street began, or, more accurately, what was left of it. This was Pogorieloye Gorodishche, a little old town. Yesterday a battle had taken place here; the pavements were dug up with craters and the houses were dotted with the scars of shell fragments as with smallpox. But these systematically demolished walls which showed empty rooms as on the stage of a theatre, these houses from which everything of value had been removed—these were not battle scars but the deliberate work of the Germans. To transform the town into a fortress, they had driven out all the inhabitants to the last man. They had dismantled the houses and used the material thus obtained for making blockhouses—many good blockhouses built according to the best rules of engineering. In these they lived for seven months, making themselves comfortable with stolen beds, mattresses, table-cloths, napkins and blankets. The Germans had not allowed the inhabitants to take anything with them—they said they needed everything. They removed picture-frames from the walls, threw out the photographs of Russian children and mothers, put their own photographs in instead, and placed them on their tables. They took a perambulator, tore off its wheels, nailed on four planks of wood, and stuffing it with pillows used it for a chair. The inhabitants were not even allowed to take children's toys; the Germans hung toys on the walls, put them on their tables. They needed everything, they found everything usable. They made themselves cozy in their new surroundings and did not expect to be driven out. They installed themselves with the arrogance of successful thieves, certain that they would never have to disgorge what they had stolen.

Now the inhabitants of the devastated city were trickling back. They made the round of the blockhouses trying to find their belongings. Their hatred was mixed with surprise. Why was it necessary to fasten wooden legs to the perambulator, to hang children's toys on the walls? What for?

At the entrance of one blockhouse stood an exhausted woman with a child whose face was as white as chalk. A kerchief was wrapped around her chest crosswise, and the child was tied to her back. The woman's hands were trembling from hunger, she was unable to carry her child in the usual way. In her palm she held the fragments of a doll—its hands, its body, its head. What had not been stolen from her house had been smashed to pieces, even this doll. She looked at me in bewilderment as though asking: can you perhaps explain this? But I didn't understand it any more than she did; it is difficult for a man to understand the psychology of apes. All I felt was that particularly malicious and wicked apes had passed through this house, much more evil and infamous than a human mind can conceive. One of these

[133]

apes, long-legged, dirty, and at last dead, was now lying at the entrance to the blockhouse, its hairy hands widespread and I was pleased at the sight. I was glad that it was lying here, that the woman kicked at it as she left the blockhouse, that there was a great deal of this carrion littering the town, that people were spitting at their beastly dead faces and that cars were crushing them under their wheels. Tomorrow they would be removed, because they would begin to stink, tomorrow for the last time someone would touch them with disgust—with disgust because these were not the bodies of soldiers, but the bodies of murderers; not the bodies of men, but the stinking carcasses of beasts.

Along the streets walked the returned inhabitants. Horrible grief had distorted their features, horrible hunger had dried up their faces. Their skin was as yellow as parchment. Nothing seemed left of their faces except their eyes—immense, full of bitterness and hatred. How they had waited! You must see them to understand the intensity of their waiting. Our soldiers, despite the barbed wire, the blockhouses and the guns that separated them from their countrymen, must have felt what was going on in the hearts of those who had remained behind the German lines. It was doubtless because they felt it that Political Instructor Gadjev and his men did what they did when a German bomb destroyed one of the links of the pontoon bridge our regiment was using to cross the river, this morning. They jumped into the water and began to fish for the planks. Fighting against the current and afloat they held these planks connecting two spans of the bridge while our infantry crossed it. They must have felt that their countrymen were waiting, that not one minute must be lost at this river.

We were at the edge of the town, near demolished houses, amidst ashes and ruins. Suddenly the woman who was telling me of her terrible life during these seven months raised her head and looked into the distance, looked for a long time without moving. I, too, looked but I did not see anything in particular, just the evening sky, a soft reddish sunset, green meadows and dark patches of woods that seemed to be drawn with a pencil, so sharply were they separated from the evening sky. But she kept on looking for a long time. And suddenly she said in a very low voice: "How beautiful . . ."

Only then did I realize that after these seven months she was noticing this familiar Russian landscape for the first time. For seven months she had looked at the sky without noticing the sunset or the dawn, the meadows, woods and green trees. She had only suffered and waited. Her soul had lost all feeling for her own land. And now that we were back she could look and again see the sky and the earth, and say involuntarily: "How beautiful . . ."

The road stretched on, across fields and woods. Hurriedly built trenches could be seen in the hollows to right and to left. The Germans dislodged from the first line of their fortifications had tried to entrench themselves while retreating to the second. They had scattered in the woods and dug themselves in. Days passed in bloody engagements. Once you have given up ground, you have to pay with blood to get it back. This cannot be helped; the price of retreat must be paid. Here and there small mounds rose above the grass: soldiers' graves with little tablets: "Here died heroically . . ." Who knows, perhaps this Red soldier was killed because seven months before someone had turned his back to the enemy at this very spot.

A path led through a field of rye. On both sides high stalks were swaying in the wind. The Germans had driven out the inhabitants of this region, but they needed bread for themselves and during the summer they brought people here to do farm work. But the Germans would neither reap nor eat this rye.

An old man walked along the path. He was returning home heavily laden. He carried a bundle and an old wooden chest on his back. Yet he stopped and without putting his load down touched the stalks: "Good rye," he said. He touched it knowing that it would be his, now.

The next village: Kubinka. Only a few houses remained here, the rest was just a mass of smoking ruins. The Germans had not had time to burn it before retreating, but today they had set it ablaze with incendiary bombs thrown from planes. In this village there were emplacements for heavy guns, and today the surviving inhabitants were walking about underground. Little children were playing at the entrance to the German blockhouses.

I have seen many a sight on the roads of war but I will never get used to the spectacle I saw there. Some day perhaps a great artist who wishes to express the depth of the national grief and the horror of this war, will paint a picture showing these ruins: a blackened brick chimney, burned planks, among which are scattered the remnants of the belongings of the people who had once lived there: an iron stove peppered with bullet holes, a twisted bed frame, torn clothing; and a thin old man, his face dark with grief, wandering aimlessly amid these ruins, picking up a rag or a fragment of iron from the ground and throwing it down again with the tired gesture of someone who has lost everything. Today I saw this old man in flesh and blood. He stood before me leaning on a gnarled stick. He looked at me and raising his trembling head, said: "If you had only come a month earlier . . ."

He repeated these words a few times, and I realized that there are no more bitter words on earth. If we had come a month earlier, his wife, Praskovia Ilnichna, would not have died of starvation, and his daughter, Natalia, would not have been shot by the Germans for going to the next village without a permit to get some scraps of food for her starving mother. And he repeated, over and over again: "If you had come only one month earlier . . ."

The next village, Mikhalkino. The Germans had not

had time to burn nor bomb it—they only looted it. Smashed windows, torn out flooring, trampled vegetable gardens.

I went out on the field beyond the village. Twisted, long-muzzled German guns stood in camouflaged emplacements. They pointed their mutilated muzzles to the sky, they would never fire again. And next to one of the guns was a plow which had traced one furrow and for some reason had not completed the other. Perhaps the plowman had been killed, perhaps he abandoned his work when the Germans came and hid in the woods. The plow had been lying there for a long time, it was covered with rust and dry lumps of earth a year old. But this Russian plow will one day complete the furrow it began. And the rust will gradually be rubbed off by the black, life-giving earth. And the plowman will return—if the old one has been killed, his son will return.

Conquerors in Captivity

✸✸✸

AT FIRST SIGHT this *sublocotenente*—which is Rumanian for second lieutenant—seemed no more than twenty-two years old. He was slightly wounded and was being bandaged. Ceaselessly, with untiring zeal, he saluted and bowed to his captors, the Red Army officers, soldiers and medical assistant. He was overanxious to show his good will, like a man with a guilty conscience. True, he did not yet know that a package of staff papers which he had thrown out of the car had been found and brought here, but he saw us speaking to the soldiers captured with him, and this perceptibly alarmed him.

These soldiers were not of his company, nevertheless they might tell us something about him, and he

[139]

made vain efforts to catch the drift of the conversation that was going on at the other end of the room. His alarm was not unfounded.

"He's not in our company, but everyone in the battalion knows him," said Private Andrea Kostaki. "He's a beast, a real beast. Now he's acting tame, because he's a prisoner, but don't trust him."

"Did he beat his men?"

"Did he beat them?" Kostaki was sincerely astonished by this question. "How could he have commanded his company if he hadn't beaten them? But he beat them so dreadfully that the whole battalion talked about it."

The private stared with hatred at the *sublocotenente*, who was groaning after his treatment; he distrusted his groans, his show of tameness, his readiness to answer questions. And Kostaki was right. Once captured, almost all Rumanian officers immediately become metamorphosed into extremely garrulous and courteous individuals. No, they didn't want this war, they are against the Germans, they've always been against them, they are at bottom Anglophiles. They're sorry that their soldiers are being killed by the thousands in this war, which they did not want any more than did their own common soldiers.

All torturers and hangmen, once they are deprived of their clubs, show themselves to be cowards. This rule applies to Rumanian officers too. And when we hear their declarations, it is difficult to distinguish

[140]

between those who are inspired by animal fear for their own skins and those who are speaking the truth. For there is a grain of truth in the assertion that many Rumanian officers are against this war. Perhaps they wanted it some time ago, but they don't want it now, when the approaches to Odessa are literally piled up with mountains of Rumanian corpses, when one routed division after another is reduced to the size of a regiment, when they can see with their own eyes that the Rumanian army is being physically exterminated. Major Bada Marin, commander of a tank battalion, and Captain Ignat Petri, staff officer of the 14th Division, spoke in that sense, when questioned. Incidentally, the major when captured had on him an interesting document, a semi-official reprimand from the commander of the division concerning the disorders in the major's battalion, and an order to form two companies of the eight tanks remaining in the battalion after their last engagements. And Captain Petri wrote a letter to the Rumanian officers: having seen the enormous losses suffered by his own and other divisions, he urged the officers to oppose continuation of the war with all their strength and to save what remained of the Rumanian army. "My only fear," he said, "is that if things continue as they are going now, all the addressees of this letter will be dead before it reaches them."

Thus speak the officers. Their statements are a combination of truth and falsehood, but what we hear from hundreds of Rumanian privates who have been taken prisoner breathes the most authentic truth.

"How were you captured?" we asked Petro Iacomi, of the 6th Rifle Regiment.

"Last night you opened an attack. Our captain was killed, many others were killed, some fled, but we remained hidden in the corn."

"Did you resist?"

"What for? Why be killed? It's better to be captured," he said with a wide gesture of his hands. "I haven't had enough to eat for a month."

"What did you eat yesterday?"

"Yesterday? Yesterday I ate nothing at all, we were attacking."

"And the day before?"

"Same thing." He seemed to recall something, and hanging his head, said in a toneless voice: "When we crossed the Prut, a few men of our company jumped into the water and drowned. They did it deliberately. They were fed up with this dog's life."

"Then why do you fight?"

"We're afraid of the Germans. If the Germans weren't planted all over our country, we wouldn't fight. Until we reached the Prut, the Germans marched with us, but after that they stayed on the other side of the river, behind us, and they sent us up ahead."

Had he fired on the Russians? Of course, orders are orders, but he doesn't think he hit anyone because during his entire training period he had practised on the firing grounds only three times.

"You're a private, aren't you? Have you received any decorations?"

"No, in our army only those get medals who march behind and fire on those who have no medals. It's not pleasant to be a prisoner," he added with a sigh, "but I thank God that I am one. At least I am alive and I am not hungry."

Private Ion Baganescu is of the same 6th Riflemen; he, too, was taken prisoner that night. In what circumstances? He knew what was up, and when his company began to retreat, he hid in a ditch and later surrendered. Why should he sacrifice his life when he has a wife and three children who have nothing to eat even while he is alive?

"You're wondering why I am so dirty? That's because of the war, and chiefly because since our arrival at the front we've received just this much soap," he spread his fingers apart one inch.

"The life of a Rumanian soldier is no bed of roses," declared Vassili Pop of the 35th Infantry. "All we get is bread made of fifty per cent corn flour and a stinking soup, and we're thankful if we get it every day. I was captured last night, and the morning before the captain slapped my face three times because I supposedly didn't answer him when he called me. Antonescu is a liar, he promised that Rumania wouldn't fight but would only conclude an alliance with Germany. Then we were told that Odessa had been taken and that we were merely marching behind the Ger-

[143]

mans. Then it turned out that in fact the Germans were marching behind us."

"I don't know how things are at home," said Private Joseph Urdea, of the 30th Infantry. "And my folks at home don't know how things are here, because if you tell the truth in a letter, the letter doesn't arrive. We were warned that all we could write in our letters was: I'm alive, in good health, and will return soon."

"How did you happen to be captured?"

"I was lucky: I was sent out on reconnaissance, and I was alone. When I saw Red Army men three hundred yards in front of me, I raised my hands—that's all. They saw and captured me."

Stephan Mardar, of the 35th Infantry, recalls his lieutenant with hatred. "The day before yesterday," he says, "he hit me in the face with all his strength because I lagged behind my platoon. I couldn't walk any faster because my feet hurt." Mardar suddenly smiled. "And then I saw that many others lagged behind and that some of them couldn't be found for three weeks. I made up my mind to do as they did."

"Did you read the Soviet leaflets?"

"Yes, I did. I read them myself and read them to others, because, you know, most of our men are illiterate—they pick up the leaflets, but can't read them."

These prisoners can be believed, because in many cases their words are confirmed by their deeds. The day before yesterday a large group of prisoners was brought to headquarters, guarded by only two Red

[144]

Army men. Rumanian prisoners have never yet made an attempt to escape. After all, they didn't surrender only to escape. The guards brought a note from the commander of a Russian unit in which he recommended special treatment for two captured artillerymen who had surrendered, turned their gun against a German battery and fired upon it.

We had a talk with these two artillerymen, Kurlan Skurlat, from the village of Krivitsa, and Georgi Kostandish, from the village of Barna, two Moldavians, old soldiers, of the class of 1909, serving in the 10th Riflemen of the 15th Division. They were in the complement of an anti-tank gun. Kostandish tended the horses, Skurlat handed the shells to the gunner. Their gun was surrounded. They saw that the Rumanian troops were retreating, that many of them had been killed, and that the others were fleeing, but they remained by their gun and decided to go over to the Russians. They were only two, because the commander of the gun had been killed and the other members of the crew had fled.

They knew the emplacement of the German battery, one verst behind them, so by their joint efforts they turned their gun around and prepared to fire on the Germans. Meanwhile the Russians arrived. Kostandish and Skurlat raised their arms and, when they were surrounded, they asked the Russian major for permission to shell the Germans. Their request was granted, and they began to fire.

"Well, how did you make out?"

[145]

"Not so badly. We had never fired before, we had only had a few lessons in firing, but we managed to handle our gun properly."

Did they hit their target? we asked. Of course, they said. After all they knew the exact location of the German battery, the same day they had gone there to get a supply of shells, so how could they miss it, how could there be any question about that? They fired for an entire hour. And the Russian commander himself told them that they were doing very well.

Would they fight against the Germans now? And how! they exclaimed. Because of these Germans they had been suffering for many months, and they knew from recently mobilized neighbors of theirs that their families were starving, reduced to begging.

Thus speak Rumanian soldiers, peasants from Rumania and Moldavia, who were forced to go to war as cannon fodder for the Germans.

One after the other the prisoners were questioned at headquarters. And in the course of these interviews we cleared up one thing that had been puzzling us. The Rumanians often attack in close formation, marching shoulder to shoulder, like White Guard officers during the Civil War who launched "psychological attacks" (one of these was very well shown in the film *Chapayev*). These attacks end lamentably: cut down by machine-gun fire, the Rumanian battalions are invariably forced to take flight, leaving mountains of corpses behind them. We noticed that in recent days there had been a number of such "psy-

[146]

chological" attacks. And yet in its general performance the Rumanian army could not be accused of foolhardy courage or contempt for death.

From our prisoners we learned the key to this paradox. The Rumanian officers are often afraid to send their units ahead in dispersed formation, because their men take advantage of it to detach themselves from their officers, hide and surrender. Only by drawing them up in a dense column and putting machine guns behind them, can their officers send them into an attack.

Death for Death

★★★

THAT MORNING ALARMING NEWS REACHED US from Arabatskaya Strelka. Commissar Nikolaev gave orders to transfer a fresh company by boats to the threatened spot. He himself crossed over on a small motor launch.

Once ashore, we learned that during the night a company of fascists equipped with motorcycles had crossed over on boats to this narrow, sandy tongue of land east of the Crimean peninsula. Our garrison, squeezed in from two sides, had perished in an unequal struggle. The Germans, taking advantage of the darkness, had moved forward and were stopped only four hundred yards from the naval battery set up on railroad platforms. Our marines who were serving

[148]

the battery decided to exact a high price for their lives. They had turned the guns and met the attacking infantry and motorcyclists with a point-blank barrage. The Nazis, leaving their motorcycles and guns behind, abandoned a farm they had occupied, retreated a mile and a half and took up a position in trenches they had wrested from our garrison.

But the situation remained dangerous; there were still no troops in front of the battery. From the high shore on the other side the Germans kept the low, sandy tongue of land under a terrific barrage from minethrowers, which prevented us from returning to our trenches. The space of a mile and a half which separated us from the enemy was only sand, with a few bushes here and there; it was open on all sides, and every inch of it was under enemy fire. Yet action was urgent, for at any moment the Germans might send over considerable new forces. Our commissar took command of the company and, stumbling heavily in the sand that yielded under his feet, he led it to the assault.

The Germans were silent. We advanced, dragging our rifles, hurrying and waiting tensely for the explosion of the first mine. We walked two hundred, five hundred, seven hundred yards—the Germans were still silent. It was hard to walk in the sand. Our men licked their dry lips with their dry tongues and, gritting their teeth stubbornly, continued their advance.

Only at about half a mile from the enemy trenches

did the minethrowers open fire, all at once, systematically. Mines were exploding along the entire front. The smoky, black explosions hid our men from each other's view.

The company was going into battle for the first time; some of the men kept moving forward, others, unable to stand the strain, pressed themselves to the ground. Suddenly an explosion roared quite close to us. I dropped to the ground, like the fighters marching beside me. When we raised our heads, we saw the commissar about ten steps ahead of us. Through the smoke and dust he was marching forward in his unhurried heavy stride, as though hammering nails into the ground with his feet. He walked calmly, carrying his tommy gun with ease. Seeing him behave in this fashion it was impossible not to get up and follow him. He walked as though there were no other course possible than to go forward, simply and calmly just as he was doing. And the men lying beside me must have had the same feeling, for we all got up and followed the commissar, involuntarily trying to imitate him, to walk as calmly, quickly, and at the same time unhurriedly, as he did.

Another five hundred yards, and machine guns joined the minethrowers. Again some of our men dropped to the ground. The commissar bent over one Red Army man and quietly tapped him on the shoulder.

"Hello, my boy! Can you hear me?"

The prostrate soldier raised his head.

"Why are you lying on the ground?"

"They're shooting."

"That shouldn't bother you. You see, I'm standing up."

"They're shooting hard, Comrade Commissar," said the soldier getting up.

"What did you think—that there would be no shooting at the front? That's how it will always be: you move forward, and they fire at you. That's what wars are for."

Now the "boy" was going forward, following the commissar and encouraging others. Half an hour later, the Germans were wiped out, and our company had occupied their trenches.

Only now, after having occupied these trenches, did we fully realize what had happened here during the night. The Germans had sneaked up in the darkness from two sides. Our infantry had accepted battle. It had been fierce and unequal.

On the dunes near the shore, at the edge of the trench, lay three corpses. Two of them lay side by side: the political instructor with his legs cut off by a machine-gun volley and a medical assistant. Apparently the medical assistant had decided to save the political instructor at the risk of his own life. Carrying his unconscious body on his shoulders he had crawled along the shore. The Germans caught up with them and barbarously cut them down with bayonets. So there they lay, pressed closely to each other, inseparable even in death.

A few steps further there was a third body, that of a Red Army man. Our blood froze in our veins when we saw him. He must have defended himself to the last, or perhaps have killed a German officer—at any rate, his resistance must have cost the Nazis a high price, for in their rage, they had laid the gravely wounded Russian on the sand near the shore, poured gasoline over him from a motorcycle tank and set him on fire alive after having gouged out his eyes with a bayonet. He lay before us, terrifying to behold, his body charred, with bloody holes scorched by the heat in place of eyes. He clamored for vengeance, for ruthless immediate vengeance against these scoundrels who do not even deserve the name of beasts. Some of them lay beside him. We saw their caps strewn on the sand, with their emblem of skull and crossbones, we saw their black armbands with the inscription "Adolf Hitler" torn by our bullets and their uniforms spattered with their ignoble blood. Yes, ignoble blood—not the blood of soldiers, but the black blood of degenerates and sadists.

They had succeeded in removing some of their dead; others remained. A senior lieutenant of the Elite Guards lay there, his plunderer's hands outspread. A bullet had pierced his head. From the pocket of his uniform protruded a copy of the *Voelkische Beobachter*. We opened it. The last page was filled with black crosses informing its readers of the destruction of a whole gang of bandits on the Eastern Front.

Beside the senior lieutenant was a motorcycle smashed by a hand grenade. All sorts of trash had fallen out of its sidecar, pieces of bread, a roll of thin yellow leather, packages of cigarettes—apparently the contents of a package destined for Germany. Well, another package would fail to reach the *Vaterland*, and another cross would have to be printed in the *Voelkische Beobachter*. We sat in the trenches reconquered from the Germans and listened with pleasure to the whizzing of the heavy shells from our naval battery which was smashing the enemy minethrower nests.

Crawling out of the trenches one by one, the Red Army men examined the body of their burned comrade. "Yes, look, look well," said the commissar. "Look and hate, look and be ruthless!"

And these men who had just completed their first attack looked, and their hearts were filled with enough anger and hatred for ten, a hundred, a thousand attacks, as many as are needed to crush and wipe out these Storm Troopers and Elite Guards, this vermin which disgraces the earth with its presence.

A cold wind began to blow from the coves. A routine night of battle followed a routine day of battle. The commissar gave orders to check all our battle posts. Whenever necessary, he himself went into the inferno with head upraised, contemptuous of death, but opposed to any useless sacrifice.

[153]

"Don't sleep at night," he said; "under no circumstances must you fall asleep."

The Crimean night, black as soot, fell upon us, demanding acute alertness to every rustle in the sand, every splash in the water.

A Woman Spy

✚✚

TODAY A POORLY DRESSED WOMAN was brought to headquarters. She looked about twenty-eight years old—perhaps thirty. Her head hung pathetically to one side, her eyes were downcast and her whole aspect was pitiable. She had been stopped by our patrols the night before when she crossed over to our side from the opposite bank occupied by the Germans. She said she had fled from there taking with her only a small bundle of clothes. Now, at headquarters, she vehemently complained of the Germans' conduct, cursed them, and cried with joy at being at last among "her own people."

Our soldiers openly sympathized with her and, before sending her on to headquarters, had given her a good meal. A soldier was carrying her bundle for her when she arrived. And many of the boys expressed regret that the regulations required sending the woman to headquarters and that she could not immediately join her family who, she said, lived "right over there, just down yonder."

At headquarters, her bundle was examined first. It seemed to contain the most ordinary objects—yet they were not those a woman would take when going on a long trip. We were forced to conclude that the contents of the bundle were less important to this woman than the fact that she carried a bundle, any bundle—a woman with a bundle is more likely to be taken for a refugee.

"How did you get here?" she was asked.

"I crossed the bridge. It is not entirely blown up, it only sank into the water."

This was true.

"But how did you manage to get by the German sentries?"

"There were no sentries at the bridge."

This was false. During the day our scouts had detected Germans patrolling the bridge. It was absurd to suppose that it would be left unguarded at night.

"But where were the German sentries placed?"

"On the hill."

"If so, they must have seen you."

"They did see me, they even called after me. But I began to run. They fired at me, but I hid below, and later managed to cross the bridge."

[156]

This was a lie, too. Our scouts had watched the bridge all night and had not heard a single shot.

The questioning took three hours. Step by step, the suspect was compelled to unmask herself. She did not admit her guilt all at once, she made several attempts to confuse us, to throw us off the trail. The first variation of her confession was that a German officer had stopped her at the well, threatened her with a revolver and ordered her to cross the river and find out the disposition of our troops. In the course of the examination, the officer soon became a couple of officers, the meeting at the well became a visit to the German kommandantur, and the threat with a revolver—a promise of a reward of five thousand rubles. It also turned out that the woman had a German pass to facilitate her return and an accomplice who had helped the Germans recruit other spies. In the end, the whole story was as clear as day. This story is instructive and worth telling, if only as a lesson to those who are inclined to premature sympathy and trust.

Anna Ivanovna Petrovna, twenty-seven years of age, was a daughter of a rich *kulak* of the Dnieper region. In 1929 kulak prosperity collapsed; Anna Ivanovna concealed her origin and somehow managed to remain in her village. In 1932 she made the acquaintance of a son of another rich kulak, named Kostiukov, who had fled to escape deportation. Their acquaintance became a close friendship, based on their common hatred for the Soviet people and their common regrets over their lost privileges. Kostiukov often

[157]

made trips. He even managed to enlist in the navy and served there four years. Soon after the opening of hostilities, he disappeared.

The Germans occupied the town in which Anna Ivanovna lived at 4:00 P.M. At 6:00 P.M. the same day, Kostiukov knocked at her door. He knocked loudly, like a man who feels at home. They had a talk. She learned that, at the first opportunity, Kostiukov had gone over to the Germans and, accompanying them, he was now trying to renew old connections everywhere and recruit spies. He suggested that Anna Ivanovna, too, "do something to help the Germans," who, he said, "would reward her substantially."

The following night Kostiukov returned, this time with two German officers. They drank together and had a long talk in a mixture of German and broken Russian. Kostiukov was producing his "merchandise." The Germans looked at Anna Ivanovna, patted her on the shoulders and obviously approved of her. After the "bosses" had departed, Kostiukov told her that he had recommended her to them as his assistant. She was familiar with the country in this neighborhood, and her first job would be to cross over to the Russian side of the river and bring back some information. Kostiukov did not fail to mention the reward she would get.

"How much?" Anna Ivanovna had asked in a business-like way.

"Five thousand," Kostiukov had answered.

She thought this was a goodly sum of money and a

[158]

sufficient price for treason. All night the two con-
spirators discussed the details of Anna's trip and,
when morning came, they went to the Kommandantur.

For half an hour Anna sat in the antechamber,
while Kostiukov parleyed in the office. Then the
woman was called in. A German officer who spoke
broken Russian handed her a pass that would permit
her to cross the bridge in both directions. During the
conversation he repeated the attractive words "five
thousand rubles," in Russian, several times. Kostiukov
then proceeded to give her detailed instructions. She
was to cross the half-sunk bridge during the night,
reach the Soviet advance posts, pretend to be a fugi-
tive, spend a few days in the region, gather information on the disposition of the troops and, most important of all, discover possible places for tanks to
cross. Then she was to return and get her reward.

But Anna Ivanovna won a reward she had not bar-
gained for.

The Traitor

★★★

JUNKERS WERE CIRCLING over Feodosya. The Germans, unable to regain the initiative, bombed the little resort with impotent rage, aiming at its white buildings, its boardwalks and the ruins of the old Genoese fortress.

The glass panes in our house had long ago been smashed, the window was covered with plywood which shook from explosions almost every minute. Shivering, casting side-glances at the window, still trembling for his life, there sat before me in the cold room a peculiar creature, who had once been a human being—ex-burgomaster of Feodosya, Vasili Sofronovich Gruzinov.

I want to tell the story of this traitor, not because

his conduct was unprecedented, exceptional, but for the very reason that he was an ordinary scoundrel and coward. Although there are fortunately not many like him in our country, these low creatures who call themselves men can be encountered from time to time. They are ready to commit any infamy, including treason, in order to preserve their miserable lives, their three rooms full of chattels, china and clothes.

I saw before me a man who was no longer young, wearing a jacket buttoned up to the neck, a worn-out leather coat and an old *kubanka* stuck on his head at a rakish angle. Not so long ago he had dressed quite differently. The leather coat, jacket, and *kubanka*—a disguise intended to give him the appearance of a guerrilla—were hurriedly put on at four minutes past midnight, when our troops broke into the town. He wanted to save his infamous life once more.

During the night he was seized by the inhabitants and brought to the commander's office. The proper authorities had not yet had time to question the mayor. He was captured, that was the main thing; for the time being there were more important matters to attend to. Thus it came about that I was the first to question him.

Strange as it may seem, he still hoped for salvation. He thought that since he had survived these twenty-four hours, he might survive another twenty-four hours, and another. All his life now was composed of such days. To cling to life, not to let it go, to live only a little bit longer! The day before I questioned him he had spent writing, covering page after page with ink. He tried to write as much as possible, to create the illusion that he had repented, that he had become useful, that he knew something for the sake of which his execution would be postponed another day, another two days.

Gruzinov was thirty-nine years old, but he had aged so much during these last two days, his cheeks had grown so hollow, that it was difficult to believe he was less than fifty. He twisted on his chair trying to look me full in the face. He did not realize that I was a war correspondent, not a public prosecutor. He stared at me fixedly, greedily, trying desperately to find some words which might prolong his life.

He was a native of Crimea, born near Bakhchisarai. In recent years he had become an expert on vegetables, fruit and wine growing and had held the job of warehouse director. In 1939 he had even tried to join the Party—he was a candidate for Party membership. In addition to being a coward, he was impudent. According to him, he had become mayor only to preserve his precious life for the Party!

But why hadn't he left the Crimea? I asked.

He had not had time. He was caught in the meshes of his fruit-and-vegetables enterprise like a captain on a sinking ship. He was ordered to destroy all the wine stores before leaving.

Well, had he destroyed them?

"Yes, that is, no, not quite. He had accidentally poisoned himself, fallen sick. He had had to keep to his room, not far from the wine cellar."

And where was his family?

Here. His wife was German, named Sofia Eduard-ovna Zimmer. She had gone to Gelendjik, but returned, because the war in the Crimea was over.

So he thought that the war was over, and that was the most important thing of all. He hoped that the Germans would not persecute him because his wife was German, and that he, as an expert on fruits and vegetables, would be able to lay his hands on the wine stores which he had so successfully failed to destroy. He hoped that now he could become a little capitalist, that he could have money and workers under his or-ders who would fear him and would not dare remind him that he was a thief and a traitor.

The Germans came to him on the very first day of the occupation to ask for the wine. Since he had so providently preserved the wine stores, he succeeded in satisfying their demands and maintaining good re-lations with them. Moreover they did not know that he had applied for party membership.

The following day he was visited by Herr Kurt, di-rector of the German agricultural department, and his interpreter.

"I don't recall his name," he added apologetically, "but if I ever see him, I won't fail to point him out to you."

He quickly looked into my eyes, he wanted to know whether it was important or not that he was able to point out the interpreter. Perhaps we would search out this fellow with the ex-mayor's help, and he would thus gain a three days' reprieve from execution.

Herr Kurt, then, had come to him with an interpreter, but no interpreter was needed, for his wife could speak German. They quickly reached an agreement. He was appointed supervisor of the stores, that is, not supervisor, but director. That was what the Germans called him: "Herr Direktor." Even now as he repeated this title his pleasure in the words, "Herr Direktor," was obvious.

Then he had made an inventory of the wine stock, and everyone was very satisfied. After that, the Germans came to him with notes from their authorities. When anyone came without a note, he refused to give him wine. He even had a telephone installed in his office so that he could ring up the commandant whenever necessary, for the Germans liked order. For that very reason, that is, for the very reason that he was reliable and conscientious, his real "misfortunes" began. On December 12, he and his wife were called before the German commandant, and he was asked to become mayor of the town.

"What was your reply to this proposal?"

"I said that I wouldn't be able to handle such a job, that I had never before held a similar post."

It seemed that this was the only thing that bothered him: he was afraid that he would not be good enough for the job, that he would be unable to justify the commandant's trust in him.

But his wife told him emphatically that he should not be afraid, that he would surely manage; and then he agreed.

What had he done as mayor? Hadn't he countersigned orders for the execution of many inhabitants of Feodosya?

"No, of course not, what an idea!"

At the mayor's office such papers were not countersigned at all, his job was only to draw up lists. The shootings were the business of the German commandant.

But was he aware what the lists were for?

"I could only guess."

Yes, he had only guessed, but this accursed degenerate who, with his own hands had drawn up the bloody lists, first of nine hundred and seventeen persons, then of two hundred and thirty. It was not his fault, he didn't shoot them, others did.

What had he done besides draw up lists?

Nothing in particular. He paid out money to the various departments of the city government and read reports on unreliable elements. The German commandant sent him these reports for comment, and his job was to pick out the particularly unreliable people.

Had he picked them out?

"Yes."

What had happened to these unfortunates afterward? He couldn't answer that question, it was none of his business. He just sat in his office, as a paid consultant of the German authorities. He sat there and wrote little notes that smelled of blood. It was a good thing the paper was white and smooth and that the blood did not stick to his fingers.

Had he seen the gallows in the town and the corpses of those shot as a result of his lists?

No, he hadn't seen them, he didn't go anywhere outside his office. He only wrote. This fact seemed to him an important extenuating circumstance. No, he hadn't seen his handiwork, for he was afraid to walk in the town, he was afraid to leave his office, he was afraid he would be spat upon, have stones thrown at him, be shot in the back, he was afraid of every one of the twenty thousand people living in the town, whom he had betrayed, each and every one.

Every morning he was driven in a car from his apartment to the German commandant to receive his instructions. Then he drove to the municipal office and labored in the sweat of his brow until late at night. At night a car was again sent for him and he again reported to the commandant. Then he was driven home. He traveled in a black sedan, with his collar raised, all shrivelled up in his seat, trying not to look out of the window. He was terrified by this silent town which seemed dead.

He felt like a stranger—because during that month he had forgotten that a Russian mother had borne him and he felt even more like a stranger than the Germans themselves. With them he oppressed the population and along with them he feared their vengeance.

The career of this traitor was broken off on the night

[166]

of December 29. That night, as usual, he had driven home from the commandant's office. But the next morning the car hadn't called for him. That morning, surrounded by a crowd of citizens, pushed and kicked from all directions, he made his last trip from his home to the commandant's office on foot. The German commandant lay dead at the door, near his car, which had been smashed by a hand grenade. And in the office sat a Russian commandant—a broad-shouldered sailor with a Mauser stuck into the belt of his leather coat.

The mayor stepped across the threshold. One of the women who accompanied him called his name from behind and he turned around. She spat in his face. Now he was sitting before me, wiping his face, as though still trying to wipe off the spit.

Again, somewhere in the vicinity, there was the report of an exploding bomb. Once again he shivered, this petty, miserable coward. Tomorrow or the day after, when he would be stood against the wall, he would doubtless weep and cling to the guards' hands. A disgusted guard would strike down those clinging hands with the butt of his rifle and he would be killed like a dog, killed as all his kind will be, killed, sooner or later, all of them to the last man, those who were caught yesterday at Feodosya, and those who are caught tomorrow in Odessa, Kiev, Smolensk. I don't know when they will be caught, but I know that they will be, that it cannot be otherwise.

Road Westward

****

THE OLD TRAIL FROM RIAZAN TO MIKHAILOV—Epifan—Bogoroditsk . . . ancient Russian towns whose names can be found in chronicles dating from the time of the Tartar invasion. . . . Our ancient Russian soil—the heart of Russia.

Once again Russian troops are marching along these old roads, driving out the foreign invaders, ruthlessly exterminating them because only a week, a day, an hour ago these invaders polluted and burned everything we had built on this soil with our own hands.

The village of Papadino, half-way between Riazan and Mikhailov, was the farthest point of the German advance. Near the road was a car smashed to smithereens. Here, German motorcyclists overtook the chief

[168]

of the district militia, a village militiaman and the village doctor (a young woman), shot them and smashed their car with hand grenades.

A little house on the outskirts of the village. Near the fence two of our scouts were buried. They were the first to enter the village. They knocked at the door of this house. The owner, an Austrian who was captured by the Russians during the first World War and had stayed in Russia, who had been eating our bread for twenty-five years, was entertaining a few German motorcyclists. When our scouts knocked at this door, he hid the Germans and let the scouts in. A minute later they were treacherously killed by a burst from a tommy gun through the window.

These were the first casualties of our attack. Later, our troops shot the traitor, buried the two scouts and continued their movement southwestwards, recapturing village after village from the Germans.

On the road we encountered more and more abandoned German trucks, motorcycles, staff cars, guns.

Mikhailov. The town had been shattered by the artillery battle. There was not a single house in which windows were intact. The crêche, the municipal library, the school—everything was defiled. The floors were littered with pieces of charred furniture, with singed remnants of books that the Germans had used for fuel. The enemy had despoiled the town but had had no time to burn it to the ground. General Golikov's units launched a violent assault on the German garrison from two sides and, at night, when the mercury stood at 30 below zero, stormed the town. After a furious night battle in the streets, the Germans fled. Their cars were in front of every house. Packages of documents littered the streets. At one intersection, stretching their muzzles toward the sky, stood their abandoned anti-aircraft guns. The enormous mouths of eight-inch guns yawned from gullies half covered with snow. The Nazis had not had time to remove the locks from most of their guns, and beside them lay boxes with live shells.

Guderian's order to burn all the cars had not been carried out. Some had been hastily damaged, others were intact. Corpses of German soldiers and officers were strewn amidst abandoned equipment, piles of stolen goods, shell cases, diaries and letters—there was an enormous amount of paper with German writing upon it.

Hidden Germans were still being pulled out of cellars. They tried to escape, disguising themselves as Red Army men, workers, even women. But their attempts were vain. Even when they ran southwestward along the roads or across fields for ten, fifteen, fifty or one hundred miles, they could not catch up with their units which had been rolled back farther and farther, toward Gremiacheye, Epifan, Bogoroditsk.

A blizzard was sweeping the ice-encrusted ground. The snow was piled so high on the ground that it was almost impossible to find the road. To right and to left were black spots—cars, trucks and tanks abandoned by the Germans. They had been left for various reasons:

some lacked gasoline, others had gotten stuck in the snow, still others had suffered some minor damage which there was no time to repair. No time, because the Russians had followed on the heels of the retreating armies, giving them no respite.

There was a particularly large number of abandoned trucks which had served for the transportation of the famous German motorized infantry. One could imagine the bitter quarrels over every seat in the trucks that had taken place on this road.

Gremiacheye is an ancient village spread out along the main road. At the entrance to it, near the first houses, was a hastily dug German graveyard. Several hundred birch crosses topped by helmets had iron or wooden plates with inscriptions in black paint. Thus the Nazis had buried their dead during their offensive. When they began to retreat they had no time to put up crosses. Twisted corpses littered the roadside. . . . But enough of them. I do not wish even to speak of them. These dogs had found the end they deserved. Everything was in order. As for the crosses—we will dig them up and remove them from our roadside as well as the helmets that adorn them. We respect soldiers and soldierly death, but we do not and will not respect thieves and murderers nor their dirty graves. They must not expect to be pitied while they live nor remembered when they die.

In the same village of Gremiacheye, the inhabitants had not yet buried fifteen of their relatives and neighbors whom they had just taken down from the gallows.

[171]

These people had refused to be German flunkeys. They had conducted themselves with the dignity befitting a Soviet citizen, and for that reason the Germans hanged them and forbade their friends to remove them from the gallows.

The town of Epifan, that is, what was once the town of Epifan and what will again be the town of Epifan. Yes, it will be! For they will be wiped off the face of the earth, this German vermin, these murderers, plunderers and rapists, and the Russian cities they destroyed will rise from their ashes as they have risen before and will stand in the same places where they have stood for centuries.

But now Epifan no longer existed. Only a few skeletons of half-ruined churches towered amidst an enormous mass of charred buildings. Night was falling. In the semi-darkness little flames of the waning fires licked out here and there along the ruins. The smell of smoke was almost unbearable. Yet, following our troops, former inhabitants of the town immediately returned. There they stood, clenching their fists, staring at the remnants of their homes, their eyes dry with hatred. They came back to live and work there. And until they rebuilt the city, they would work in its ruins. The Germans have not been able to conquer us by the fire of their guns and they won't conquer us by burning our cities.

Strong and enduring is the Russian people. Strong and enduring, but terrible in anger. I traveled along devastated roads, through villages burned to the ground, through places where the cup of suffering, it seemed, had overflowed. Yet I saw few tears. When you hate strongly, you have no tears. When your deepest desire is for revenge, you don't weep. When, beside the charred remnants of your home, you see an accursed enemy corpse, not a sob but a triumphant shout rises to your throat.

For ten days now General Golikov's units had been advancing, fighting fierce battles. Alferievo, Serebrianye Prudy, Mikhailov, Gremiacheye, Epifan. In certain sectors, our divisions had advanced one hundred and fifty miles in these ten days. Every day fifteen miles of reconquered land, our own Russian blood-drenched land.

Beyond Epifan the Germans built trenches and escarpments, poured water over the slopes—all in vain. Our fighters rushed forward, took the trenches, stormed the escarpments, despite their ice-covered sides, and defeated the enemy in pitiless hand-to-hand fighting.

Below Gremiacheye, the Germans threw tanks and armored cars into the fray. Our infantry stood still, met their blow, repelled it and continued their advance. These peasants from Penza and Riazan, these workers from Tula and Gorky, marched forward, across the icebound fields, through winds and blizzards, fighting their way from house to house, from village to village, from town to town.

Night. Amid the snowstorm immense fires filled the horizon with their glow. The retreating Germans

[173]

burned everything they could, everything they had time to burn, everything that happened to be around. They seemed to have lost all hope of returning, they wanted to slam the door definitely.

We continued to drive southwestwards along the road. Then we came upon an enormous fire—it was Bogoroditsk burning.

A short stop at the village of Konduki. Everything was burnt. The Germans had left only a few hours ago. Red flames were still twisting their tongues above the houses. Off to one side, on a hill, four houses had escaped the fire. All the surviving population of the village had gathered in these houses. Frost-bitten, starving women with babies at their breasts had spent the last two nights in the fields, hiding in haystacks and snowdrifts. Now, through the smashed windows of the houses on the hill they watched the flames consume the remnants of their homes.

An old woman asked us in a hurt voice to wait until she could prepare some potatoes for us.

"They wanted to burn our potatoes, too, those monsters," she said. "They opened the cellar and tried to burn them, but the potatoes just didn't want to burn, and here they are. Please, dear, dear boys, please stay a little while and eat. God knows how many days you've been marching in the cold just like us. And let me wash the table for you, don't sit at it now, it's befouled. As soon as the Germans came in, they used to light a lamp, undress, sit naked on the table and squeeze their lice. Manka!" she called to her daughter, "get me a knife. I must scrape the table with a knife, those scoundrels have so befouled it it'll make you sick at your stomach to sit at it."

After Konduki, Kolodeznaia. The Germans had left this village even more recently, only a few hours ago. Once again, charred chimneys, ruins, women and children huddling in barns, shivering with cold.

Two Germans were brought before the commander —they had just been captured near a house that had escaped the flames. They had not succeeded in running away and, having despaired of escaping, they decided, like the wolves they were, to finish the work begun by their fellow gangsters. They were captured with straw in their hands, about to set fire to a house.

Could these murderers and fire-brands be called prisoners of war? Is there any human word to describe them adequately? A bullet in the head was all they deserved. They were taken to a spot twenty paces away from us, near the ruins of a burnt house, and shot. They fell writhing on the snow that was blackened by ashes. Such was the end of their infamous lives. Our men marched off without turning their heads. Everywhere there was the smell of fire and smoke. Filthy carcasses littered the blackened snow.

And Bogoroditsk was still burning. The artillery was thundering, and when the wind was silent for a moment one could hear the incessant rattle of machine guns. The blizzard was so dense you couldn't see more than three steps ahead of you. Tonight Bogoroditsk must be taken. Perhaps it was already taken, but we had had no report of it as yet. General Golikov sent one of his staff officers to find out about it.

"Comrade general, what is the password for today?" asked the officer.

"The password? It is Bogoroditsk. You hear me? Bogoroditsk. And the answering word is Bogoroditsk, too. And don't come back without the news that it is taken. Understand?"

A few minutes later, the commander vanished into the blizzard. The thunder of the guns came closer and closer. Now the entire horizon was one huge glow, and even the snow flying in huge flurries seemed red against this background.

In the morning, our units led by Colonel Nemudrov broke into Bogoroditsk. The streets were smoking. Here and there stood an isolated house that had escaped the fire. In one of these houses our men found seven half-dressed German soldiers who had gotten drunk the night before and slept during the battle. This would have been impossible in July, unlikely in September, but now it was possible. They stood there blue and shivering with cold and fear. They were afraid they would be shot. But they were not shot, although, in all justice, they deserved no other fate. Only a few minutes ago our men had found fourteen Red soldiers locked up in a cellar and burned alive.

Two guards led the seven Germans along the streets of the burnt city. They led them far away behind the lines, through burnt cities and villages, through ruined towns. They brought them to the prison camp that was their destination, for such were the orders. But they would have been happy to stick a bayonet into the throat of every one of those ignoble gangsters before they had gone three steps. Our men would lead them through burnt villages, through lines of women who cursed them and spat in their faces. They would have to defend them from the popular anger, from old men who would gladly have hung them on the nearest tree or strangled them with their own hands. When the Red soldiers entered a hut to warm themselves they would have to take those seven scoundrels with them, those same Germans who only a day or two before had stolen everything they could from this same hut and hanged its owner from the beams. The Red Army men would bring them where they had been ordered to bring them. But I don't know which of us would have been the first to raise his hand against their guards if they had not protected them.

I was in a house two-thirds of which had been burned—only one room remained. Beside me, on the window sill, sat a five-year-old girl with a serious, old woman's face and hollow cheeks and eyes.

"Well, Rayechka, tell me, what did the Germans do here?"

"They took the little blanket."

"Whose blanket?"

"Mine. And they took grandmother's socks. And grandfather's socks, too."

A tall old man got up in the corner.

"We thought they had taken everything. The

blanket hung on the window. They were on their way out when they saw it and dragged it down. And it could hardly be called a blanket, it was so small—more like a handkerchief. But no, they turned back and tore it down, too."

The old man's voice was trembling with anger, with anger and surprise. He had lived many years and he couldn't understand how people could reach that degree of savagery.

"No, they are not human beings, they are not human beings," he repeated with conviction, shaking his gray head. "I can't call them human beings, I can't."

No, they cannot be called human beings. They cannot and must not.

I was taken back to headquarters in an army plane. From above we had a particularly good view of those burnt towns and villages, those collapsed roofs and charred chimneys—the handiwork of scoundrels who dare call themselves human beings.

The roads were littered with their tanks and cars. Many of them were lying there—but not enough. We want more, more of them, to the last machine.

The ditches along the roads were littered with their corpses. There were many, many corpses—but not enough. We want more of them, to the last man.

We landed in a village. Tearing off his helmet, the pilot of the liaison plane said in a dull voice: "I can't stand this any more. I'm going to ask to be transferred to an attack squadron. I want to kill them with my own hands. I want to feel them dying."

[178]

Yes, he was right. I understood him perfectly. I had the same desire, every one of us who has seen all this has the same desire: to kill them with our own hands, at least one of them, but with our own hands.

December 1941

The Third Adjutant

THE COMMISSAR BELIEVED that brave men were killed less frequently than cowards. This was his firm conviction. He expressed it again and again and was angry when anyone contradicted him.

He was loved and feared in the division. He had his own method of training men for war. He studied a man while walking with him. For a whole day he wouldn't have him out of his sight; he'd take him to divisional and regimental headquarters and anywhere else he happened to be going. If he were going into battle he'd take his man along, marching at his side. By night, if the man had passed the test satisfactorily, the commissar went through the formalities of making his acquaintance.

[180]

"What is your name?" he would suddenly ask in his abrupt voice.

The startled officer would give his name.

"And my name is Kornev," the commissar would say, holding out his hand. "Kornev. We have walked together, we have been lying on our stomachs together, and now let's get acquainted."

A week after his arrival in the division, two of his adjutants were killed. The first took fright, climbed out of his trench at a critical moment, and tried to crawl back. He was cut down by machine-gun fire. That night, on his way back to headquarters, the commissar passed his dead adjutant by without so much as a glance. As for the second adjutant, a bullet had passed through his chest in an attack. A low autumn sun sent its last rays straight into our eyes. The air was cold and intolerably dry. The wounded man lay in a re-captured trench, gasping and begging for a drink. There was no water around. In front of the breastworks German bodies were scattered. Near one of them, a canteen lay on the ground.

The commissar took out his binoculars and looked through them for a long time as though trying to see whether the canteen was full or empty. Then he la-boriously moved his heavy body—he was no longer a young man—to the other side of the parapet and went along the field in his usual unhurried gait.

For some mysterious reason the Germans did not open fire. They began to shoot only after he had come near the canteen, picked it up, shook it, placed it under his arm and started on his way back. One bullet hit the canteen. He stopped the hole with his fingers and walked on, holding the canteen with both hands. He jumped down into the trench and carefully, so as not to spill the precious liquid, handed the canteen over to one of the soldiers.

"Give him a drink!"

"What would you have done if the canteen had been empty?" someone asked.

"I would have returned and sent you to find another, a full one," the commissar replied, with an angry look.

He often did things which a divisional commissar is not usually supposed to do. Later, he would be angry with himself and anyone who reminded him of such acts.

After bringing in the canteen, he didn't go near his adjutant. Absorbed as he was in watching the battle-field, he seemed to have forgotten all about him. Fifteen minutes later he suddenly asked the commander of the battalion: "Well, did you send him to the medical post?"

"It can't be done, Comrade Commissar," said the commander, "we must wait till dark."

"He'll be dead by then." The commissar turned away, considering the conversation closed.

Five minutes later, two soldiers bending down to dodge the bullets were carrying the adjutant's motionless body across the hilly terrain. It was perhaps unreasonable, but when the commander of the battalion asked, "Who will carry him?" the soldier who had seen

[182]

the commissar get the canteen, said "I." After what they had seen, they couldn't help it. The commissar looked on coolly as they passed. He applied the same yardstick in measuring danger for himself and for others. Men die—that's what war is for. But brave men die less frequently.

The Red soldiers walked courageously, without throwing themselves on the ground, without forgetting that they were carrying a wounded man, and for that very reason he thought they would arrive safely. At night, on his way to headquarters, the commissar stopped at the medical post.

"Well, how is he, have you fixed him up, is he recovering?" he asked, with his customary abruptness. He thought that in wartime everything had to be done quickly: transmission of reports, execution of attacks, curing the wounded. And when the surgeon told him that his adjutant had died from loss of blood, the commissar raised his eyes in surprise.

"Do you realize what you're saying?" he said in a low voice, taking the surgeon by his belt and pulling him close. "Our men carried him a mile under fire so that he could live, and now you say he's dead. Then what was the good of carrying him?" He failed to mention the fact that someone had exposed himself to fire to get the adjutant a drink of water. He failed to mention this, not because of modesty, but simply because he had forgotten it.

The surgeon shrugged his shoulders.

"Besides," said the commissar, perceiving the gesture, "he was a brave fellow, and he should have lived. Yes, he should have," he repeated angrily. "You don't work well!"

And he went to his car without saying goodbye. The blue spots of the headlights flashed on the black trunks of the cypresses. The car turned to the left and disappeared. The surgeon stood in the doorway for a while. Of course, the commissar was wrong. Logically, what he had just said might even have been stupid. But in the commissar's words, in his angry and sad voice there was something so strong, so convincing, that for a minute the surgeon thought that brave men actually should not die, and that if they died it was because he did not work well.

"Nonsense," he said aloud, trying to dispel the queer thought. But the thought did not leave him. He seemed to see the two Red soldiers carrying the wounded man across an endless hilly field.

"Mikhail Lvovich," he said suddenly to his assistant, who came out on the porch for a smoke, as though merely remembering something he had decided long ago, "tomorrow morning we'll have to set up two new medical posts nearer the front lines . . ."

The commissar didn't reach headquarters till daybreak. Outside there was a drizzle mixed with snow flurries. The foul autumn weather was setting in. The commissar was in a bad temper and dismissed the men he had to see with brief, grumbling exhortations. He acted thus not without method. The commissar liked people to be angry when they left him. He believed that there was nothing a man couldn't do, and when he scolded someone, it was never for something he could have done and didn't. When a man did something big, the commissar reproached him for not having done more. He was firmly convinced that a man thinks better when a little angry. He liked to break off his sentences half-way, so that only his main intention was understood, and the rest left to be worked out by the other. By such tactics he made his presence constantly felt in the division. He could not be with everyone all the time. But when he spoke with a man, he tried to give him enough to think about until the next time.

In the morning he was given a list of the losses suffered by the division the day before. Reading it, he remembered the surgeon. Of course he had been tactless in accusing the experienced old doctor of doing his work badly, but what did it matter, let him worry, maybe he'd get angry and think up something useful. He didn't regret what he had said. The only sad thing was the death of his adjutant. But he didn't allow himself to think of that. If he did, there would be too many men to remember. He would remember them later, after the war, when unexpected death would again be a misfortune or an accident. For the present, death was always unexpected; there was no other kind of death, you had to get used to it. And no doubt because he was sad despite all this reasoning, his voice was uncommonly dry when he informed the chief of staff that his adjutant had been killed and that he needed a new one.

His third adjutant was a small, fair-haired fellow

with blue eyes, who had just graduated from school and was at the front for the first time. On his first day with the commissar, when he had to walk out with him to the battalion across the frozen field amid bursting mortar shells, he never lagged behind for a moment. He walked close beside the commissar, because that was his idea of an adjutant's duties, and also because this big corpulent man with his unhurried gait seemed to him invulnerable—as though walking beside him would protect a man from any mishap.

When the mortar shells began to explode with increasing frequency and it became clear that the Germans were aiming at them, the commissar and his adjutant flung themselves on the ground from time to time. But no sooner had the smoke cleared away than the commissar would get up and move on. "Forward, forward," he grumbled, "there's no point in staying here."

Close to the trenches they were "straddled," one shell exploded in front of them, another immediately behind. The commissar got up shaking the earth off him.

"You see," he said, pointing at the crater behind them, "if we had been frightened and had hesitated, we would have been hit. Always move quickly forward, then nothing will hit you."

"But if we had walked away faster . . ." the adjutant, instead of finishing his sentence, merely nodded at the crater in front of them.

"Not at all," said the commissar. "They aimed at us

here, and the shell fell short. If we had been there, they would have aimed closer, and their shell would have been short just the same."

The adjutant smiled involuntarily; of course the commissar was joking. But then he realized that the commissar's face was serious and that he had spoken with conviction. And suddenly the adjutant felt that he had faith in this man, the kind of faith that in time of war is born in us suddenly to remain forever. For the last hundred paces he walked very close to the commissar, elbow to elbow; now he knew that it was impossible for this man, or anyone who walked beside him, ever to be killed.

Such was the first day of their acquaintance. A month went by. The roads to the south were frozen one day, muddy and impassable the next. Unharvested grapes rusted and rotted on the vines. The deserted fields were furrowed with trenches. There were rumors that somewhere in the rear new armies were being prepared for a counter-offensive, and meanwhile the thinned division carried on bloody defensive battles.

It was a dark autumn night. The commissar was sitting in a mud hut; he moved his wet, mud-spattered boots closer to the hot iron stove. That morning, the divisional commander had been seriously, no doubt mortally, wounded. The chief of staff almost noiselessly drummed the table with his fingers. He was pleased that he could do it; the fingers of his wounded

[187]

hand were still bandaged, but they were beginning to obey him.

"You're a stubborn man," he resumed the conversation after a brief interruption. "I'll grant you that Kholodilin was killed because he was scared, but our general was a brave man, or would you deny it?"

"He *is* a brave man, not 'was.' And he will survive," said the commissar, and as was his custom turned away, considering the matter settled.

But the chief of staff pulled him by his sleeve and said in a low voice, so that no one else could hear his sad words: "Well, suppose he does live. But Mironov didn't live, nor Zavodchikov, nor Gavrilenko. They all died, and they were all brave men. How do you fit them into your theory?"

"I have no theories," the commissar said brusquely, "I just know that if everything else is equal, brave men die more rarely than cowards. And if you never stop mentioning the names of brave men who died, it is because when a coward dies he is forgotten even before he is buried, while we speak and write about the brave men who died. We remember only the names of the brave, that is all. And if you insist on calling this a theory of mine, you must admit that a theory that helps people not to be scared is good, and that other theories are bad. Incidentally, this theory helps me not to be afraid, too," the commissar smiled suddenly. "To tell the truth, we ourselves are scared sometimes, too."

The adjutant entered the mud hut. In the last month his face had darkened and his eyes had grown tired, but otherwise he was still as boyish as on the day the commissar had first seen him. Clicking his heels, he reported that on the peninsula he had just visited everything was in good order, except that Senior Lieutenant Poliakov, the company commander, had been wounded.

"Who has replaced him?" asked the commissar.

"Lieutenant Vasiliev of the third platoon."

"And who is in command of the third platoon?"

"Some sergeant."

The commissar thought for a while.

"Are you very cold?" he asked the adjutant.

"Yes, to tell you the truth."

"Have a drink," said the commissar, pouring him half a glass of vodka. The adjutant hastily unbuttoning his coat drained the glass at one gulp.

"And now get back there," said the commissar. "I am worried, you understand. I want you to be my eyes on the peninsula. Get going."

The adjutant rose. He buttoned his coat slowly, as though to enjoy a few more moments of warmth. But once his coat was buttoned, he stopped dallying. Stooping low so as not to hit the ceiling, he vanished in the darkness.

"A good fellow," said the commissar. "He is the kind that I think nothing can happen to. I think that they will come through unharmed, and they think the same of me. And that's the main thing. Isn't it, colonel?"

The chief of staff continued to drum on the table with his fingers. A brave man, he did not like to reduce his own courage or that of any other man to any theories. But this time it seemed to him that the commissar was right.

"Yes," he said. "And more generally I don't believe that anyone dies at all. I always think that someone will always take the dead man's place and will make no worse a job of it, and for that reason I believe we will win, because if it is really so, we must win."

The wood crackled in the stove. The commissar slept with his face on an opened map, and his hands were spread out wide over it, as though he were trying to recapture all the enormous territory desecrated by the enemy.

The next morning the commissar went to the peninsula, crossing the estuary in a fragile boat. A strong north wind was blowing and high, white-crested waves struck the boat with a roar.

Later he did not like to recall that trip. The night before, the Germans had made a sudden landing on the peninsula and after a fierce battle wiped out the entire third platoon to the last man. During the day, he had to do things which, as a commissar, he was not really supposed to do. In the morning he rallied every available man and three times led them to the attack. The sandy terrain was pitted with craters and drenched with blood. All the Germans were killed or captured. Those who tried to reach their own shore by swimming were drowned.

The commissar gave someone his now useless rifle with its bloody bayonet and made the rounds of the peninsula. Only the dead could tell him now what had taken place here the night before. The dead, too, can speak. Among the German corpses lay the Red soldiers of the third platoon. Some lay in the trenches, stabbed by bayonets, clutching their smashed rifles in their dead hands. Others, who had taken fright, were lying in the open field. They had run away and were overtaken by enemy bullets. They lay with arms outspread, their faces turned to the east and their backs to the enemy. The commissar walked slowly on the battlefield, examining the attitudes and the petrified faces of the dead. To him, even in death, these men were divided into brave men and cowards. From a dead man's attitude he guessed his conduct in the last minutes of his life, and even death could not reconcile him with a coward. If he had had his way, he would have given orders to bury the brave and the cowards separately.

He carefully examined every face, trying to find his adjutant. He knew that his adjutant could not have fled or surrendered, he was here, somewhere among the dead.

At last the commissar found him all the way back, far from the trenches where men had fought and died. The adjutant lay flat on his back with one arm clumsily bent under him, the other out-stretched and gripping a revolver. On his chest there was a cake of blood.

The commissar stood over him for a long time, then he asked one of the officers accompanying him to open his tunic and see whether the wound on the adjutant's chest was from a bullet or a bayonet. He would have done it himself, but his right arm, wounded by shell fragments during the attack, hung useless at his side. He was irritated by the sight of his tunic cut to the shoulder and his hastily tied, blood-soaked bandages. What angered him was not so much his wound or his pain, as the very fact that he was wounded, he whom the division regarded as invulnerable, whose invulnerability gave the men additional courage in battle. His wound was something out of place, something to be cured and forgotten as soon as possible.

Meanwhile the officer had opened the adjutant's tunic and shirt. "It's a bayonet wound," he said, raising his head toward the commissar. Then he bent down again. For a long minute he lay close to the motionless body. When he rose, his face showed surprise. "He is still breathing," he said.

"Breathing?" The commissar displayed no sign of emotion. He did not know yet whether to be concerned about this man who turned out to be alive. He lay here far from the trenches and had doubtless fled. And yet—no, he could not have fled. Scarcely ever had the commissar been mistaken in his judgment of people.

"Two men here," he suddenly said in a commanding tone. "Take him to the ambulance at once. He may survive." And he went on to continue his round of the battlefield.

Would he live or not? In his mind the question was confused with another question: how did he conduct himself on the field of battle, why had he turned up behind everyone else? He could not help thinking that if he had been brave and conducted himself well, he would live, he would surely live.

That was no doubt why, a month later, when the adjutant, pale and thin, but still as fair-headed, blue-eyed and boyish as before, returned from the hospital to divisional headquarters, the commissar asked him no questions, but silently held out his hand, the one that had not been wounded.

"I never did reach the third platoon that night," the adjutant began. "I got stuck on the crossing, and I had only a hundred paces to go when . . ."

"I know," the commissar interrupted him, "I know everything, you don't have to explain. I know that you are a brave man and am glad that you have recovered."

He looked with envy at the young man who, only a month after receiving so dangerous a wound, was again fit and healthy, and, pointing with his eyes to his own bandaged right arm, he said in a subdued voice:

"But the colonel and myself are no longer young. It's the second month and my wound hasn't healed yet; and his wound is three months old. We command the division with one hand each—he with his right, and I with my left. Though, as a matter of fact, the results aren't bad . . ."

A Visitor from Norway

"I'll take the first one on my cutlass, and you take the second," said our commander and he pressed close to the wall at my side.

"When the door creaked and a tall, ruddy German entered holding a rifle in front of him, the commander stooped and spread his legs to keep his balance. With one hand he gripped an iron bracket that was nailed to the wall, with the other hand he plunged his cutlass into him . . ."

Erik Christiansen stopped speaking and took a deep puff on his little black pipe. He had not smoked for a long time and now he kept packing his pipe with numb disobedient fingers, striking match after match and puffing. He sat near a round iron stove in a mud hut on

<caption>[194]</caption>

the Rybachi Peninsula; he was warm, wearing my sweater and the artillery captain's trousers, while his own clothes, still wet with sea water, dried hissing over the fire.

Christiansen was tall, lanky, fair-haired, with a face burnished by wind and frost, with knotty hands capable of rowing for forty-eight hours on end, with long nimble legs which had walked far and wide, all along the coastline from Kirkenes to Narvik.

That night, with Yorick Svensen, the schoolteacher, he had crossed the stormy Barents Sea in the face of a furious gale. In a fragile boat, sailing or rowing, he had crossed the sixty miles separating Rybachi Peninsula, in Russia, from the northern coastline of Norway.

He spoke Russian well, for thirty-nine years ago he had been born here on Rybachi and had done a good deal of fishing with Russian fishermen. And yet, though he often used characteristic Russian seacoast idioms, he spoke like a foreigner, because he was a Norwegian and from the age of fifteen had lived in Trondheim, Varde-fiord and many other good places to which he now could return only at the risk of being hanged on the first tree.

He had just arrived, he had a great growth of beard on his chin, and he was numb with cold, but he was in a hurry to tell us all he had seen in his last months of wandering amid the cold cliffs of the Norwegian coast.

"And so the commander took the German on his cutlass," he went on, puffing at his pipe, "but he had

[195]

been wounded in the leg near Varde-fiord in October, and he slipped on his wounded leg and fell on his knee. Then I bent over him and took the second German on my cutlass. Then we pulled both Germans inside, slammed the door and bolted it. The door was big, thick, covered with cast iron, and it couldn't be opened easily.

"We circled the house and all four of us gathered in the kitchen. From the window we saw that after the two Germans who died silently upon entering this house, eighteen soldiers had alighted from a large covered truck, while an officer and the driver remained in their seats . . .

"At this moment we were sorry that there were only four of us and that Knut Larsen wasn't there, because he alone was worth four other men, and if there had been eight of us, we could have killed all these Germans.

"I forgot to tell you about Knut Larsen. He died three days before we got into that little house on the seashore. Knut Larsen was a fisherman from Trondheim, and our commander liked him more than any of us, because he deserved it. He was killed on Saturday. Yes, yes, on Saturday. That was in the morning, in the village of Helpao, three miles from Kirkenes. The forester, Skoelle, lived there, and we often dropped in to see him because we trusted him and also because we needed to warm ourselves from time to time. It has been a cold fall and we couldn't spend the whole time in our hut. Knut Larsen went to see Skoelle on Saturday. Two men from Kirkenes were supposed to be there that day and report what people were talking about in town and whether a big troop ship was due soon—as a letter from Trondheim had led us to expect.

"The two men arrived on time and sat down at the table with Knut Larsen and Skoelle. They ate dried fish and drank beer; it was Skoelle who got the beer for them. Then they asked Skoelle to leave, because, although they trusted him, he was not supposed to know everything they knew. And Skoelle left. They sat for another half-hour and were about to leave for good when Knut Larsen thought he heard someone walking under the window. But the pane was covered with frost and you couldn't see anything outside. Then Knut Larsen—he always liked to see everything for himself—opened the door slightly and looked out into the street.

"All around the house there were German soldiers. They stood calmly with their rifles and laughed because they knew they had surrounded the house and that no one could get away.

"But Knut Larsen thought differently. He shouted to the two men from Kirkenes to follow him, and he himself, firing his revolver, rushed past the German soldiers. Now they stopped smiling, raised their rifles and began to shoot. One of them was in Larsen's path, but Larsen hit him in the chest with a knife and went on running. The three men had reached the first rocks, and in four more minutes they would have disappeared from sight, but at this very moment a bullet hit Larsen

[197]

in the back. He fell on the snow and shouted to the two men from Kirkenes: "Run!" They ran because if they, too, had been killed, no one would have been left to tell us about the troop ship that was coming from Trondheim.

"But Larsen was a strong fellow, he sat up, bracing himself with his two hands in the snow, and turned toward the soldiers who were running toward him. They had stopped firing because they thought they would take him alive. But Larsen didn't want to be taken alive; he had a hand grenade on him, but it was hard for him to get at it because he could sit up only by bracing himself on both hands. He clenched his teeth, bent to the left, supporting himself for a second on his left arm alone, while he got his hand grenade with his right. The hand grenade was loaded, it needed only to be shaken. Once again he leaned on both hands, but in his left he held the hand grenade. He waited for the soldiers to come closer; when they were quite close, he put all his weight on his right hand, shook the hand grenade without dropping it, and banged it against the icy ground.

"The two men from Kirkenes saw Larsen die, and they heard the cries of the wounded soldiers. We learned of Larsen's death and we also learned that the big ship from Trondheim would never reach Kirkenes . . .

"And now, in the little house on the seashore, Larsen was not with us, and that's why there were only four of us, and we decided that if we remained in the house

[198]

we would be burned, so we went out to meet the Germans when they approached. But we didn't go out all together. Only two of us had revolvers; the commander and I only had cutlasses. The commander had told the two with the revolvers to go out first and shoot from behind the stone wall until the Germans killed them. Then the Germans would think there was no one left in the house, they'd come in through the open door. The commander and I would hide behind the door and each of us would take a German on his cutlass, and with luck, even two Germans, each. And once again the commander said he was sorry that Larsen wasn't with us.

"The two with the revolvers went out and stood behind the stone wall. The soldiers spied them almost at once. But there were many of them and they were not afraid. They advanced firing their rifles. Our men fired their revolvers, and three soldiers fell before reaching the wall. Then we stopped watching and hid behind the door so as not to be seen by the Germans.

"There was still shooting behind the wall, and we stood keeping our knives in readiness. But suddenly the commander told me: 'Christiansen, I will stay here alone, and don't argue, for I'll kill you if you do. I've just remembered that over there near the fiord Yorick Svensen and Matissen and two others are waiting for us. If the soldiers kill all of us they'll go over there and kill the others, too. So, run, Christiansen, those are my orders. But give me your cutlass.'

"I gave him my cutlass, and he gave me his, and said:

'If you ever see my daughter, give her this knife; she's a good girl. And now, run.'

"I left the commander and began thinking how to escape. I went out on the other side of the house, and crawled along the wall, out through the gate, and then again along the wall, and then I ran on the snow.

"I didn't see what was going on on the other side of the house, but there was still shooting, and when I began to run across the snow the Germans didn't see me. But then they sighted me—not the soldiers near the house but the officer and the driver who had remained in the truck. When I looked back, I could clearly see the officer firing at me with a rifle which he had set down on a fender. He fired several shots without stopping, but only later when I was near the sea did I realize that one bullet had pierced my leather jacket and embedded itself in my sweater. All night I walked along the seashore and not until morning did I reach the little fishing village where Yorick Svensen and the others were waiting for me.

"I told them everything that happened, and we went on to a hut we knew along the shore. For three years no one had lived there, except for ourselves off and on.

"Yorick Svensen waited for the commander to decide what to do with Skoelle. The day before, fishermen had come from the village of Helpao and told them that Skoelle must have informed on Knut Larsen, for he had come back from Kirkenes with a bag of flour which he could only have got from the German commandant and not from any Norwegian, because the Germans had taken all the flour long ago.

"But the commander wasn't with us, so we decided by ourselves—there wasn't much to decide anyway. We separated, and two of us went to Helpao to kill Skoelle.

"Yorick Svensen and Matissen and myself stayed on; there was no place for us to go until we had made contact with the others. We had only a little boat which couldn't hold the sea in such weather, but just to be on the safe side we stowed a barrel of drinking water in it, and if we had had any food we would have put some by, but we didn't have any. At night a fisherman came out from the village and told us that some people had gone close to the house where we had fought with the soldiers, and seen the Germans bury five of their men and put crosses with helmets on their graves. The Germans fussed around for a long time because the ground there is stony and they had to scratch it with their bayonets. And when they went to the village, all the men left because no one wanted to help them bury their dead. But when the Germans left, the villagers returned and buried two of our men who lay there.

" 'Two men you said?' I asked the fisherman.

" 'Yes, two,' he said.

"Then I realized that the third man had escaped.

" 'What did they look like?' I asked him, trying to find out whether our commander was dead.

" 'They had long beards,' said the fisherman.

"But all of us had beards after wandering for three

weeks in the woods, and I still didn't know whether the commander was dead, and the fisherman didn't know him because the commander was from far away, from Trondheim.

" 'But what did they look like?' I asked again.

"Then the fisherman remembered that one of them had a thick beard and was bald. And so we learned that our commander was dead.

" 'And I was also sent to tell you,' said the fisherman, 'that the Germans have surrounded the whole district from Helpao to the sea and that they are searching for you everywhere.'

"We sat down for a while and began to think. We wanted to smoke badly but there has been no tobacco in Norway for half a year.

"Then we asked the fisherman whether he had something to eat for us. He rummaged in his pockets and pulled out two pieces of dried codfish. That would be food for one day, we decided, if we had to put out in the boat. We had no weapons, except two knives, an axe and my cutlass. And we knew that if the Germans came we wouldn't have anything to fight them with.

"But putting to sea would likely mean death too, it was just a choice between two ways of dying.

"So we waited till morning, and at daybreak soldiers appeared on the shore from two sides. They walked cautiously, taking cover between the stones. They didn't know that we had nothing to shoot at them. We went down to our boat and shoved off. As long as we were close in to shore, the soldiers didn't see us, but when we moved out, they spied us and opened fire with their rifles.

"There was a strong wind blowing that seemed to carry the bullets away. Only one hit Matissen in the back, but he didn't say anything about it until we had reached the open sea. We expected the sea to be our grave, but we didn't want the soldiers to insult our bodies, and the sea is a good grave for a fisherman.

"We hoisted our sail, and pulled it down and rowed, and hoisted sail again. On the second day a big wave washed Matissen out of the boat. He was so exhausted from his wound, he drowned before we had time to hold out a hand to him.

"The third day we landed here, Yorick and I. You can see my hands for yourselves; the skin's all rubbed off, and I've rowed all my life so it's not from lack of habit."

Erik Christiansen sighed as he looked down at his hands which wouldn't row or hoist sails for a long time to come, then gave a push to Yorick Svensen who lay beside him on the cot, and told him something in Norwegian.

Yorick Svensen sat up beside him. He was a little old man with a dark face tanned by the wind and simple, iron-framed glasses on his nose—like the glasses our old schoolteachers wear.

"Without Yorick Svensen, we'd never have gotten here," said Christiansen. "Svensen isn't a seaman, he's an old schoolteacher, but when I felt like throwing down the oars and giving up, he would say: 'Hold on, my boy, we'll get there.' He spoke to me as if I was a child, and he knows how to speak to children. Two generations of Norwegians passed through his school and thank God grew up to be good men who will put up a good fight for their freedom."

Involuntarily we cast another look at the teacher. The old man sat motionless, clasping his knees in his hands; he had clear blue eyes and many wrinkles, and if it hadn't been for his eyes, it would have been hard to imagine how he looked as a young man. But if you looked into his eyes, you couldn't think of him as old.

Catching the direction of our glances, Christiansen, too, looked at the old man.

"When the German soldiers came to Norway," he said, "Svensen was on leave at Oslo and later he told us all about it. The German consul was a confirmed hunter and often had gone hunting with our king in the woods near the seashore. The day of the invasion, when the king fled to the coast, the consul put on a colonel's uniform; he knew all the roads and trails the king could take, and followed him, in advance of the German soldiers. But it seems that near one hunting lodge an old huntsman lay in ambush for the consul and shot him down with a gun loaded with buckshot for wolves. I don't know for sure, but it must be true because Yorick Svensen told us the story, and all his life he has never told anything but the truth—to grownups and children alike."

The old man sat motionless, with bowed head, as though listening to the conversation. His head trembled a little; it seemed that he was nodding in approval.

"He has been like this since Narvik," said Christiansen. "He was a volunteer at Narvik and was twice wounded in the head. You mustn't think he is so very old. It's not his age that makes him this way, but his wound. He's a good shot, and when it comes to scrambling over rocks, he can outstrip me easily."

Christiansen was silent for a while and then added: "When we get back home, he'll be our commander. That's what I decided here, and the ones who stayed, decided the same. Yes, I'm sure that's what they decided. In fact, they think we're drowned; to tell the truth, the sea was bad . . ."

We went out of the mud hut. Christiansen thrust his broad chest against the wind. From the west, from Norway, the northern lights were rising; they spanned the whole breadth of the sky with a great bridge of light, as though joining these two solitary men who stood on our shore to their native land, so close and yet so distant, hidden behind the high, grey surges of the winter sea.

The Only Son

****

IT WAS FAR BEHIND THE GERMAN LINES in the subpolar regions of the northern front. A wet, early spring blizzard was raging.

The scouts who had parachuted down from their plane, carrying heavy loads of explosives, walked toward the bridge, but during the very first stage of their march they unexpectedly ran into a German unit. There was only one way in which they could now carry out their mission. They must steer clear of the Germans and reach the bridge at least half an hour before the enemy. Since the first thaw the rocks were completely covered with ice. The Germans advanced over the snow, now lagging behind, now sinking into drifts, now catching up with the trail left by our scouts.

[206]

Everything would have gone smoothly, if Lieutenant Ermolov had not been wounded in the very first exchange of bullets by a stray shot of an automatic—an incredible piece of bad luck such as sometimes strikes people who have passed laughing under the very nose of death a dozen times. Ermolov was hit in both legs above the knees. Here, far from all medical aid, this meant death in a few hours. He fell, then raised himself on his elbows and asked for a drink. His comrades poured him a few swallows from a flask. He cast a glance at his motionless legs, at the dark puddle of blood forming under them and said: "Leave me here." All of them knew he was right, but to leave him behind was beyond their strength. Captain Sergueev, trying not to look into Ermolov's eyes, gave the order to carry him. Ermolov was carried by two men, in turn. The other two carried the explosives. Whenever they had to negotiate a steep passage, his bearers put Ermolov on the snow, climbed ahead of him, and the other two handed him up to the first pair.

They now advanced more slowly, with the Germans close on their trail. The scouts who marched at the rear now and then crouched behind a stone, and tried to hold up the enemy's pursuit by firing with a submachine gun. After about two hours, the whole thing became senseless; they were advancing so much more slowly than the enemy that by now he was doubtless trying to outflank them and might even get to the bridge before they did.

As they were crossing a wide, snow-covered dell,

Ermolov's pain pierced his unconsciousness for a moment. He began to speak inaudibly. Sergueev put his ear close to the lieutenant's burning lips. "Nearer. Still nearer," said Ermolov.

"You have no right to do this," he was saying. And although his words could barely be heard, his voice grew suddenly hard and angry. "You have no right to do this. It's treason."

He closed his eyes. He did not want to talk.

Sergueev understood that Ermolov had used the word "treason" deliberately, to force his captain to do what he wanted him to do. Ermolov was full of anxiety about the bridge. What he wanted was necessary—horrible, but necessary. Sergueev moved away and continued to walk beside the lieutenant in silence. When they had crossed the dell, he gave orders to put Ermolov down on the slope of a small mound covered with stones. They laid him on a tarpaulin spread out on the snow. He had lost a great deal of blood and kept losing consciousness, off and on. Sergueev told the others to advance, taking all the burden of the last farewell upon himself. He unhooked the flask from the young officer's belt, drew a tin can of food out of his bag and opened it with his Finnish knife. He put the can and the flask near Ermolov's left hand. Then he unbuttoned the wounded man's holster, took out his pistol and put it on the tarpaulin so that its wooden handle touched Ermolov's fingers.

The lieutenant sat leaning against a pile of stones

that formed an angle. He watched the captain silently with calm, unblinking eyes.

Now Sergueev could look straight into those eyes. He had done everything that was necessary and just as the dying man wanted it to be done.

"That's all," said Sergueev. "Farewell."

Still silent, Ermolov pressed his hand with unexpected vigor. Sergueev strode off without turning back. An instant later his white cloak disappeared behind a jutting cliff, and Ermolov thought to himself that this was the last man he would see in his life, except the Germans who would soon be here.

His pain was intolerable and he longed to end it as soon as possible, but at the thought of the Germans his desire to shoot himself left him at once. He raised his pistol and shot into the air. He did not want his comrades to be tormented by uncertainty; let them think that it's all over and consider the matter settled. But he would go on fighting. He was glad that he had been able to cock his gun so easily. So he still had some strength in his arms—that was good. Once again he raised his pistol and aimed at a green spot of moss sticking out of the snow. He easily got it in the sight of his gun, his hand did not tremble at all. He put his weapon down.

Snow was falling. The sky was entirely covered with pale snowy clouds. The polar sun had not set, but the twilight was darker than usual. The instinct of an experienced scout told him that the Germans were bound to pass him by sooner or later. The only question was, at what distance would they notice him? He could hit them at thirty paces. He cast an anxious glance at the sky.

He was alone, entirely alone, no one could help him —neither his comrades nor his oldest friend—his father. Closing his eyes he recalled his father as he had seen him for the last time in his dugout, at headquarters. He was sitting over his artillery tables chewing a cigarette, and grumbling that the scouts were not working well, that they had destroyed only four batteries in recent months. But despite his father's complaints Ermolov knew that he worked well, that his father was satisfied with him, and that his growling was just a habit he had developed to conceal his love for his only son.

Now, in disorderly succession, he evoked various details of his friendship with his father—how his father had scolded him out without showing any sympathy for him when he fell from his horse as a child, how they had fenced with rapiers in the sports hall of the artillery school where his father then served, how the son had forced his father into a corner and how satisfied the old man was and how, for the first time, smiling into his mustache, he had told his wife to put two wine glasses on the table—"for the two men." He recalled that his father was not tender with him, that never in his life had he called him by a diminutive, but always "Alexei," how he always scolded him in the presence of friends and praised him rarely, and that only when they were alone. And suddenly, with all the acuteness of which only a man who has little time left to live is capable, he felt the desperate love, tenderness and pride that lay hidden behind his unemotional, almost cold relationship with his father. Of course, he loved his mother, but now he could not recall her gentle hands, her tired smile, nor the thin wrinkles around her eyes when she cried. She seemed very remote and irrelevant to what was happening to him. But the details he remembered about his father were important at this moment; they were part of the reason why he was lying here now with a pistol near his hand, why he had mastered the horrible pain in his legs, and why he had decided to wait for the Germans, come what might.

He had reached this decision not only because this was his eleventh reconnoitering trip and because he had accustomed himself to the idea of a horrible death, but also because from the age of four he had accompanied his father from barracks to barracks, from unit to unit; because his father had no sympathy for him when he fell from his horse; because his father had been happy when forced into a corner by his son during a fencing match; because, surely, his father could not have imagined him dying in any other way than the way he wanted to die now.

He opened his eyes and looked around. The blizzard was still raging, his legs were almost entirely covered with snow and the dark spots on the tarpaulin were no longer visible. For a second he fancied that he was a little boy lying on a bed, that the snow was a white blanket, and that his mother was about to tuck him in and wrap the blanket around his neck. I must be sleepy from loss of blood, he thought, I must rouse myself from this torpor at any cost. Clenching his teeth, steeling himself against the pain, he summoned up all his strength and deliberately jerked one of his legs. A monstrous unimaginable pain pierced his body; it was as though someone had thrust a stick through him. But he achieved his purpose, the pain dispelled his drowsiness.

He pricked up his ears. On his right, from behind the mound, came a rustling noise. "It's good that it's so soon," he thought to himself and with his left hand he transferred the can of food to his right side. Then raising his gun he placed his right elbow on the can, so that his arm would be higher and more firmly supported.

The rustling grew more and more distinct. The Germans were moving without caution—that was good. But why was he alone, all alone—if only he had two of his boys with automatics to help him. . . . "In a minute it will all be over, and no one will know what took place, not a soul, not even my father," he thought with anguish.

He set his elbow more comfortably on the can and made sure again that he could get into his sight the little green spot of moss which now had almost entirely disappeared in the snow.

The first German passed at fifteen paces, without looking in his direction. The second, who wore a dirty white cloak over his grey uniform and had an automatic rifle around his neck, stooped down to find the path, suddenly looked to the left, toward Ermolov, and uttered a cry. Ermolov pressed his elbow to the can so hard that it hurt, and fired. The recoil made his weakened hand slip down the can. Struggling, he resumed his previous position and aimed his gun at the second German who, upon hearing the shot, had turned toward him. The German's automatic got entangled in his cloak and while he was trying to disengage it, Ermolov waited. He fired only at the very last moment, when the German, having finally gotten hold of his weapon, was about to press the trigger. The German dropped his gun, stumbled forward a few steps and fell with his face down in the snow, almost touching Ermolov's legs with his hands.

From behind the slope a few shadows now seemed to be coming toward Ermolov—and because they were shadows and not men, just dark blurred spots, he realized that he was losing consciousness, and that he had to fire his last shot if he did not want to fall into their hands alive. At this very last moment he suddenly remembered his mother who had so often stroked his hair and face. He put his pistol not to his temple, but to a place under his open padded waistcoat, three fingers below the left pocket. He gripped the gun so tightly that his right hand was still pushing the pistol down as it sank into the snow.

Colonel Ermolov did not return to headquarters before morning. Because of the late spring snowdrifts he had walked the last twelve miles. Having pulled off his wet boots with a feeling of luxurious pleasure, he lay down on his low cot and smoked. A blizzard that was unusual at this season had been raging for two days. Cold blasts of air blew into the dugout, and now and then the colonel got up in his bare feet to put wood into the round iron stove. He had made his report to his superiors; the cot of the commissar who had not yet returned from divisional headquarters was empty, and an unaccustomed silence prevailed in the dugout, only rarely disturbed by the crackling logs in the stove and the roar of the wind outside.

What formerly, in peacetime, was regarded as solitude—the absence of friends, wife and son, the separation from home,—now, in wartime, did not appear as solitude. The countless numbers of men who night and day visited him as chief of the army's artillery section, his commissar, a gay and intelligent man from Yaroslav with whom he had been living for eleven months, the commanders of the regiments whom he rang up on the telephone every night—all these people filled his days, constituted his whole life and had long ago obliterated any feeling of loneliness. But today, when visibility from all the observation posts was nil because of the blizzard, when for hours at a time there was no need of telephone conversations even with staff headquarters, and when he somehow could not fall asleep, he suddenly felt acutely alone.

He tried to evoke his wife. She was now somewhere far away, in Siberia, and all he could see was only an endless string of envelopes written in her hand—some of them were still somewhere in Siberia in a mailbox, others were traveling in a train, still others were near him in the mailing department handled by unknown hands. They were all moving, traveling toward him, yet they were only letters.

But his son was there. And perhaps because he was constantly there, quite close to him, the colonel felt his solitude with extraordinary acuity. He rarely saw his son. Several months ago he had asked some old friends to assign his son to the army group with which he himself served; but for the very reason that, against his principles, he had made such a demand, he made no efforts to see his son oftener than the requirements of the service necessitated—and these requirements made it necessary only very rarely. The last time he had seen him was a month ago, in this very dugout, when he received a report from him on the results of an artillery reconnaissance deep into enemy territory. The colonel had then been happy to note that his son had a hard, masculine face, that he was calm, spoke little, and was even a trifle over-formal with his own father. At that moment, for the first time he had felt that his tender, fussy wife with whom he had had many discussions on the subject of how to raise a boy had not spoiled his only son after all, and that at the age of twenty the boy was just as he had wanted him to be, as he had himself been at that age. He had even liked his son's refusal to drink tea with him and that, standing at attention, he had asked permission to leave. He granted his request, but when the young man reached the door of the dugout, the colonel suddenly called out "Alexei!" And when the boy turned around, the father gave him a sly friendly wink, as when in his childhood he had caught him in some mischief that forecast his future manhood. In reply his son winked at him, too, and smilingly repeated his request: "May I go?"

That had been their last meeting.

In fact he loved him as tenderly and yearned for him in his absence as only fathers love and yearn, those who have an only son embodying all their hope and pride, all their faith that the son will in the end grow up to be a real man, just as they are themselves, or better. It was because he was ashamed of this, in his view excessive, tenderness, that the colonel always called his son "Alexei," although in his own mind he never referred to him otherwise than as Aliosha or Alioshka. Sometimes it seemed to him that his son needed his tenderness, sensed it, and at such moments he was particularly severe with him.

The dugout grew cold again. The colonel sat by the stove and began to throw in wood again. This iron stove suddenly reminded him of his youth, of the days when he commanded a light mounted battery under Budenny. In recent months he had become accustomed to staff work and on occasions maliciously and drily mocked those of his subordinates who liked to move forward without any real reason. But sometimes he missed the feeling of direct contact with the enemy, the rapture of battle. Out of the past he suddenly evoked galloping artillery carriages, light guns firing point-blank, hoarse cries of command, sweating faces of artillerymen, little falling figures in foreign uniforms. Now he was deprived of all that. The only time in the course of this war he had experienced anything close to the old exhilaration was in the two preceding days. A part of the army had passed over to the offensive, and the main observation post was advanced far ahead, on top of a high, jutting hill which dominated all the surrounding country. This time his duties not only permitted him, but actually forced him, to be at the main post for two days and personally direct the fire of a few brigades of heavy artillery. Their guns were firing at long range at enemy bastions and battery emplacements. But from the mountain the view was so clear that through his fieldglasses, at a great distance it is true, he could see Germans running in confusion, falling horses, wooden supports flying.

His observation post was under the fire of German batteries, he had to correct the aim of his own guns and he was stirred by the feeling of direct struggle. His commands were given in a voice that was hoarse not only from cold and lack of sleep, but also from the excitement of battle. But these two days were not likely to recur soon again. In this respect his son was luckier. The colonel would not have admitted this thought to anyone, not even to his own commissar, but he could not restrain it within himself. The profession of scout chosen by Alexei seemed to his father terrifying. His son had not asked for his approval, and he had done well not to ask for it. What could the colonel have said? Of course, he would have approved. More than that, if his son had asked to do staff work, he not only would have been angry, but would have done everything in his power to see that such a request was refused. Not that he despised staff work, that would have been stupid, but he felt that his son should pass through the same stages of development he himself had lived through; that he should not skip any of them. To remain alive on this path was his son's own business, his son's and no one else's—it was no concern of his, just as his own sleepless nights when scouting parties remained behind the enemy lines for several days without giving any news of themselves—as they were doing now—were of no concern of his son's. In fact, if the truth were told, his present sleeplessness was again caused by the thought of his son. For some days there had been no news of the scouting party, a blizzard was raging, and no one knew when it would be over.

The colonel threw the last log into the fire, sat down on his cot and began to remove his belt, hoping to get some sleep after all. There was a knock at the door.

The commander of the scouting battalion, Captain Sergueev, came in. He had obviously just come back, he still wore his camouflage cloak, unbuttoned, and his automatic was slung over his shoulder.

"What's the news?"

"Just a minute," said Sergueev, and dropping his automatic with a bang, he sank onto the commissar's cot.

[218]

Sergueev was silent, his face showed signs of utter exhaustion; the fact that he had come to the dugout immediately upon his return from his mission, when he knew there was no other assignment waiting for him, was alarming.

"Well?" said the colonel and, lighting a cigarette, he moved forward on his cot so as to face Sergueev.

"Just a minute," repeated Sergueev and slowly pushed the automatic away from him, as though it prevented him from speaking.

"Wounded?" asked the colonel.

"No, Andrei Petrovich," said Sergueev in a low voice. And less from the tone in which he said the word "no," than from his having called the colonel, for the first time in the war, by his two first names, gently, as one speaks to a sick man, the colonel understood that all he had to learn were the circumstances of his son's death.

When Sergueev had left, the colonel lay flat on his back, trying to think. But his mind was blank, only the word "Aliosha," which he had never said aloud in his life, sounded again and again in his ears. "Aliosha," he said, and then was silent. He closed his eyes, opened them again and repeated his son's name, over and over again. But his mind remained blank, there was only the grief, for which he had tried to prepare himself so many times during these long months of war, and for which, he saw now, he had not succeeded in preparing himself. To shake off this blank feeling he began to recall his conversation with Sergueev. Why had he asked him that pitiful and useless question: "Was there a note for him?" Of course not. Sergueev would have given him the note if there had been one. But why wasn't there one? At least two words . . .

Suddenly, thinking of this note and of its absence, he imagined all the details of the event: the tarpaulin on the snow, his son's shattered legs, the handle of the pistol, and that last shot Sergueev had heard as he left. No, a note wasn't necessary. He wouldn't have written one himself. Again he evoked the last stretch of road his son had walked, the cliffs over which his motionless body had been carried on a folding stretcher, the stones on which he had been left alone, all alone, or more accurately, with his pistol, a soldier's last companion. He saw his cold body and the Germans coming near him. The Germans . . . Half an hour before, Captain Sergueev, as though trying to comfort him, had deliberately recalled all the scouting expeditions in which his son had taken part, the hand grenades thrown into dugouts, the blown up bridges, the German officers he had killed. No, his grief was not lessened by all these memories. His son was his only son, and now that he was dead, there was no one in the world who could replace him. But from the thought that his son had had time to avenge his death, the father's grief, although still grief, did not degenerate into despair.

He could not help thinking of the last two days, of the soldiers running in confusion he had seen through his field-glasses, of the falling horses and the flying wooden supports, and now it seemed to him that among the violent emotions he had felt during the battles there was a premonition of his son's death, a premonition of the blow that would strike him.

He fancied that while he gave commands in a hoarse voice at his observation post, his son had been beside him, and that together they were destroying the people he hated.

No, he knew that he could not be comforted. But he knew also that despair would never get hold of him, that in spite of the immense grief that now oppressed him, he wanted just as violently as ever to live and to fight, above all, to fight.

But the mother? What would she say? ... . She could not strangle the murderers with her own hands, she could not, as he could, direct against them the long muzzles of death-dealing guns. She must not be told that her son had saved the last bullet for himself. She must not be told that her boy had not been buried by his comrades. He realized that his grief would not pass the next day, nor the day after that—that it would never pass away, and that he must write her at once, at this very table, and not wait until tomorrow, because tomorrow it would be even more impossible than today. He would write at once. She would forgive him if he lied to her.

When he had finished his letter, the rosy spring night was gone. He went out of the dugout. Beyond the snowstorm, beyond the mountain peaks the cold sun was rising. From the west came a heavy roll of guns. He looked at his watch: yes, eight o'clock sharp. Those

[221]

were his guns, they were opening an artillery offensive —the same one he had given orders to begin at eight— the day before, when he had not yet known that his son was no more.

The guns began exactly at eight—that was as it should be. The war went on.

No, it was not true that she lived from letter to letter. Sometimes it seemed so to her, but it was not true. If in this forgotten little Siberian town she had been the only one who was waiting for her husband and son, she knew her life would have become nothing but tormented waiting, because of her deep love for them. But since everyone around her—her neighbors, her colleagues at the school, and even the children in the third grade to whom she taught Russian language and grammar—was waiting for a husband or son or brother, the situation became a habit, a matter of course. She was spared the anguish which besets people who suffer alone, when those around them do not understand them. No, everyone understood her very well. And even the mischievous boys on the back benches, the "Kamchatka," knew with their childish intuition when she was upset because no letter had come for several days, and made less noise than usual. Children will always be children, and will always make noise, laugh and play pranks, but even on them the war had left its mark—almost all of them were separated from their fathers, and some also from their mothers. And like her, their schoolteacher, they could not help knowing that their common fate was being decided somewhere far away, that people were fighting and dying out there, that wounded men were arriving in the town, and being unloaded from cars near the Third School, which had long ceased to be the Third School, and was now a hospital. And all this taken together was called the "army"—a word which the children pronounced with reverence.

And Anna Petrovna was proud that the two men closest to her, her husband and son, were part of the thing which the children loved so much. Her greatest joy in the whole course of the war was a letter from her husband informing her that his request to have his son serve in the same army group as himself had been granted. From that day on, Anna Petrovna believed that her husband and son were together. She would say to her friends: "I'm glad that they're together now. That makes it less terrible, doesn't it?"

By tacit agreement, father and son, although usually far from each other, always wrote at the end of a letter addressed to her: "Father embraces you," or "Alexei sends his regards." This made her think that they were sitting together somewhere, and that her son—he was always so lazy—instead of writing his own letter had merely asked her husband to add a few words for him.

She had always known her husband, when he was young and now, in his maturity, as a decided, calm, strong man. As far back as she could remember he had been a leader of men. He had brought up Aliosha, taken care of him, and it seemed to her that now, at the front, he, so big and strong, was again in a position to watch over the boy, to protect him from all dangers. As of old, as when her son was a child, she felt that he was safe with his father. And that was perhaps why all her fears were concentrated on her husband. No matter how long an interval elapsed between Aliosha's letters, she thought to herself: "That lazybones hasn't written again," and she was a little angry, but when a letter from her husband was delayed, she soon grew worried.

She was worried right now. She was returning home from school very tired. The day had been hard. Petia Gridasov, a ten-year-old, tow-headed boy, the chief prankster of the school, had come in this morning unusually subdued, and suddenly, during the last class, had burst into tears, his head sagging on his desk. It turned out that his family had just received news of his elder brother's death at the front. She had to take the boy home after school and comfort his mother, Maria Nikanorovna, and she had asked her to tea in the evening, for it had seemed to her that the poor woman was not sufficiently comforted and that it was her duty to tell her something that very night that would make her feel a little less despairing.

Anna Petrovna was in a hurry to go home, for she had to cut some wood after dinner, prepare the samovar and iron a fresh napkin, in brief, to make everything ready for her guest.

She walked through the town. It was spring: little

green shoots were sprouting on the trees. Remembering that she had been without a letter from her husband for a long time, she thought it might be interesting to know what kind of weather they had had up there in the north, that surely the snow was still on the ground, and that they had no real nights, that it was light all the time. She had asked several times in her letters for a description of the country and the weather where her husband and son were living, she wanted to know about everything around them. But for some reason they had never answered her questions, perhaps because they were concerned with other things or perhaps only because they were men, and men don't like to write about such things.

A letter was under her door, pushed in there by her landlady who had gone out. She picked it up, slowly weighing it in her hand—the letter was long, thick— and put it on the table. Then she unhurriedly took off her overcoat, moved a comfortable chair over to the table and put on her glasses. She never renounced the pleasure of tormenting herself a little before reading a letter, of preparing herself for it. Then she read it with concentration, not thinking of anything else. And today the letter was long, she had much pleasure ahead of her—more than usual.

The letter began as usual: "My dearest . . ." Her husband had always begun his letters with this phrase, all his life, even in 1920, immediately after their marriage. "My dearest . . ."

She read the letter to the end, and pushing it away

[225]

from her, as though fearing to touch it again, she staggered to her bed. Later she realized that she must have fainted—her heart had always been weak.

When she came to, she was lying on her bed. The room was as silent as before. She sat up and because of some incomprehensible hope cast a glance at the table; for a second she imagined that it had not happened, that no letter was lying there, that it had all been a bad dream. But the letter was there where she had left it. She returned to the table, sat down again and, controlling her fear of touching the pages, picked them up. But having read the familiar first words: "My dearest . . ." she realized that there was no need to re-read the letter, that everything in it was engraved in her memory, word for word, just as it was written. And she knew that she might live another thirty years, become a very old woman, and that the letter, each word in it, line after line, would never leave her memory and would always be in front of her eyes, no matter where she put it away.

She did not remember whether she had cried or not —undoubtedly she had. No one heard her, her apartment was empty, everyone had gone out.

Her husband wrote her that Aliosha had been killed in battle fighting with his comrades to the last cartridge, that he had been brave and sold his life dearly. She recalled that place in the letter and said mechanically: "Yes, yes . . . That's good . . . Of course . . ." But it was hard for her to imagine it all, even though to the father it was doubtless very important that it should have happened in this and no other way—doubtless very important, because otherwise he would not have described it in such detail. But she could see only her son's face, his hair, his hands, his body that she knew so well, which at first was tiny and had then grown big, but which to her had never changed, from the very first day. She suddenly began to think of the place where he had been wounded—no doubt a terrible wound, all bloody. Was it his face, his forehead, which she had so often stroked and kissed? But his father wrote that a bullet had struck him in the breast, in the heart. This was surely better, the end had come quickly. But when she thought of the place where the bullet had hit him, she somehow recalled his body when he was little, so small and childish, and it seemed to her that grown-up, infamous men had murdered her child, her little child.

Then she recalled another passage in the letter, where her husband described how Aliosha was buried by his comrades, how they had carried his coffin covered with green pine branches, how they had given him a salute with their guns, and what a fine open expression he had had in the coffin, just as though he were alive.

"Just as though he were alive," she repeated those words several times. That was good, that his face was as if alive. And green pine branches around his face—that, too, was good. She wept again, her grey head sinking on the table.

An hour later, when she had forced herself to be

[227]

somewhat calmer, she was suddenly beset by the thought of her husband. She knew that he, like all men, was not at all as strong as he seemed to others and to himself. She considered herself the strongest person in the family. She was always gentle, sometimes timid, she rarely quarreled with him; he considered it his duty to comfort her, but way back in 1920, when their first son had died, it was not he who had sustained her, but she who had sustained him. Then he had wept, with his big head on her knees, and she had soothed him. She was a woman, she had suffered a great deal, but women like herself could bend and bend, but never break. But he . . . men like him, big and strong in appearance, could break suddenly. She must help him, perhaps join him and do something that would console him, for not even Aliosha knew (only she knew) how much his father had loved him. And then she tried to recall how she had comforted her husband after the death of their first son. She realized with horror that she had comforted him then by telling him that they would have another son, the same who was now no more . . . She thought to herself that she was now forty-five years old, that she could not tell him this time what she had told him then, that she could not and would not. They would not have another son, they would never have any son.

She tried to imagine their future life without their son. And it seemed to her that life would be easier for her than for her husband. Her love for him was greater and stronger than his for her—she knew that. She would transfer all her tenderness to him, she would take care of him as of a little child, she would do everything to make him think of their son less often. She would comfort him. She would have a great deal to do in her life; for many years, she would doubtless have to save him from despair, and for that very reason she would bear life more easily than he. She would find a way—she did not know how, but she would surely find some way of consoling him.

When she heard a knock at the door, she remembered at once that it was Maria Nikanorovna, whom she had invited to tea in order to comfort her. Her guest was lucky, she had another son.

She opened the door. By now her eyes were dry and her hands had ceased to tremble. She asked Maria Nikanorovna to come in, apologizing for not having her tea ready and began to attend to the samovar. The two women sat at the table facing each other, and Aliosha's mother consoled with Maria Nikanorovna in her grief without mentioning her own. This made her feel better. It seemed to her that in the same way, without mentioning her own grief, she would speak to her husband, and comfort him, suppressing her own feelings.

Her heart was now full of solicitude for the living as well as of grief for the dead.

The next morning, as usual, she entered her class at nine o'clock. She felt that she would have a hard time controlling her voice today, and for that reason she gave the children a composition, and pretended to

[229]

study the class records, while she gave herself over to her melancholy thoughts.

She felt lonely, lonely as never before. All her life she had known only how to love; she loved her husband and her son, she loved the children whom she taught at school. And now, suddenly, in the course of a long tormenting sleepless night she had learned to hate. This hatred now tormented her, because she felt helpless, because she had weak hands, incapable of taking vengeance on the murderers. Involuntarily, perhaps for the first time in her life, she clenched her fists and bent over the table to conceal her pale face. But her old, schoolteacher's habit of watching the class was stronger than she was. A few minutes later, raising her head she saw her boys. And suddenly these dishevelled, tow-colored and dark-haired boyish heads reminded her of all the generations of boys who had passed through her hands, who had scrawled their first written words under her, in the second, third and fourth grades, who later, completely grown-up, sometimes with beards, speaking in a masculine voice had come to visit her and embraced her gently and carefully, because they had grown so big and strong, and she had remained so little. They were now twenty, twenty-five, a few of them almost thirty years old.

And she suddenly thought that all these boys, or almost all of them, were now fighting. If she could now cry out to them that their old teacher's son had been killed, that she was unhappy, that she begged them not to help her, no, but to avenge her, oh, how they

[230]

would have avenged her, these children, who had become men!

But were they not now avenging her?

Before her eyes flashed the smoky battlefields, the red flames of explosions, the tanks crawling through crashing trees—all the things that she had never seen before, but saw now, suddenly, as though illumined. And everywhere, north and south, wherever the war was being fought, along those smoky fields her boys were marching, her boys in steel helmets, unrecognizable and stern, avenging her.

A Red Army man is hit during a counter-attack to rectify a wedge in the Soviet lines.

Soviet infantrymen dislodging Germans from a village.

A gun in action under enemy fire.

A nurse bandaging a soldier directly on field of action.

Reconnoitering at a river crossing.

Soviet infantrymen advance behind tanks.

Tanks and riflemen dislodging Germans in the Stalingrad area.

A trench mortar crew takes up an advanced position on the firing line.

A village on the Southern front is cleared of Germans.

Automatic rifleman fighting in village-outskirts near Stalingrad

Crawling back to his lines with a wounded
Red Army man.

A soldier carries back a wounded comrade on
his shoulders.

Supported by artillery a Soviet unit occupies a key height at the Finnish front.

Soviet seamen of the Northern fleet land on enemy territory.

A Red Army Reserve Unit at an outpost.

A reindeer inspects the wreckage of a Junkers plane shot down in the arctic region.

In a dugout at the Northwestern front.
A command post at night.

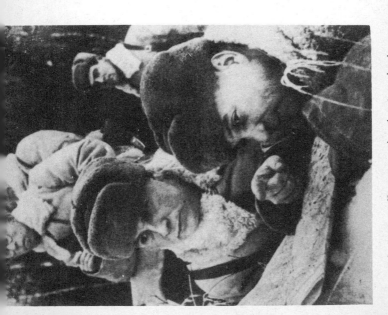

Red Army officers study the invaders' defense belt.

Peasants returning to their village liberated by Soviet soldiers.

Bodies of women killed by the Nazis and

A traitor under guard in a liberated area.

Women of a collective farm, on their way to the fields, in a liberated area near Smolensk.

German prisoners, taken in the Ukraine, on the way to prison camp.

Nazis who bailed out of a damaged transport are taken to post headquarters.

Prisoners of war on the Leningrad front.

Bodies of Germans abandoned by retreating Nazi forces.

The bodies of 77 Soviet civilians—tortured to death during the Nazi occupation of their village.

Behind the broken enemy lines, after the Red Army victory at Stalingrad.

Another of the series: a Nazi gallows and one of its victims.

A gallows in a German-occupied town. (These photos found on Germans killed at the front.)

The execution of five Soviet civilians: one of a series of eight photographs found on a Nazi officer.

Home again—Soviet woman erasing the German word "reserved."

Household crockery, buried by civilians, is dug up as Nazi loot (photograph found on prisoner).